SCHOOL BOARD LEADERSHIP
2000

—●—

The Things Staff Didn't Tell You at Orientation

by

C. Gene Royer

Brockton Publishing Company
Houston, Texas

School Board Leadership 2000
The Things Staff Didn't Tell You at Orientation

by C. Gene Royer

Manufactured in The United States of America.

ISBN 0-9638758-9-2

First Edition
10   9   8   7   6   5   4   3   2

Policy Governance™ is a Registered Trademark held by John Carver to specify his particular model for board governance.

CONTENTS

FOREWORD

Gene Royer's guide for school boards is as helpful as it is lighthearted. He has applied the Policy Governance™ model of board leadership to the domain of public school boards, an arena at the same time visible to critical scrutiny, politically volatile, exposed to constant attack – and nothing less than precious to the future of our children and even of democracy itself.

As creator of the Policy Governance model, I read those who would explain it to their specialized audiences with a measure of – let me be frank – distrust. While people have the right – perhaps even a kind of historical imperative – to create new ideas, new models, and new twists on old ones, slipshod efforts in that direction merely dilute good concepts and ravage conceptual integrity in the name of adaptation.

Policy Governance was crafted carefully to overcome most of the widespread foibles of governing boards, whether in public education or elsewhere. As a fresh paradigm of proper governance and an empowering board-staff interaction, Policy Governance represents massive change in conceiving of the board's role. For many years we have known that boards should engage themselves primarily in policymaking, that they should govern rather than administer, that their challenge is to establish vision rather than micromanage. But having said that, boards fail regularly on all these counts. The message of Policy Governance – the radical message I formulated in the mid-1970s – is that nothing short of a revolution in governance is necessary to support these purported board virtues.

Merely patching the problem areas, merely training

board members, merely – in effect – tinkering with a fundamentally flawed machine is not worthy of board members, dedicated staff, consumers, or taxpayers. Governance is too bad for fixing; it must be re-invented.

Gene Royer understands this. As an application of Policy Governance principles to public school boards, his text maintains a level of conceptual fidelity that I am pleased to see and happy to endorse. Gene's treatment of school governance will help board members who wish to avoid being super-superintendents as much as they want to avoid being rubber stamps. His book is for school boards committed to being the public's voice in the leadership of its systems of education.

I heartily applaud Gene's efforts and those of the many elected "servant-leaders" committed to transforming the governance of public education.

John Carver, Ph.D.
Atlanta

CHAPTER 1

THE PARADE IN PROGRESS

The common cliche declares that, "all a leader has to do to be seen as visionary is find a parade and get in front of it". In the realm of education, a parade of ideas is constantly in progress; and the one whose banner should be held highest is that spending money for schools that produce illiterate graduates is a not only a waste, but a travesty. If one utters that accusation – and many have – few will rise to challenge, as the cry for educational reform reverberates from all quarters of American society.

Faith Popcorn is the CEO of BrainReserve, a company hired by Fortune 500 companies to tell them the trends and fads of the future so they may have products ready and, thereby, be in front of the parade. Pertaining to public schools, she has already speculated they are likely to fail in the 1990's. They will fail not because hardworking people will lack dedication in preserving the schools' integrity, but because they will be perpetuating a quality that is already in a downward spiral. Public schools will be irrelevant to the needs of that sector of the economy which does the hiring. They will fail because someone else will do what needs to be done. And, perhaps, at a much lower cost.

A change is needed, but it cannot come from the middle of the parade. It cannot come solely from teachers, and it cannot come solely from superintendents. It must come through more effective governance. Only the board has the superior position and opportunity to alter the character of public education and set it on a new course. – To say, "This is the new route the parade will take; these are the avenues we will strut down first; and it is now time to *strike up the band."*

In his book ***Boards That Make a Difference*** (Jossey-Bass, Inc.), John Carver, PhD., expresses his concerns for the design of today's board governance process and presents a better way.

Two decades ago, when he first began advocating the governance model of his creation, called Policy Governance™, boards of nonprofit and public organizations were finally given the opportunity and courage *to see themselves as others see them.*

To some, the sight was not a pretty one, as Carver's relentless evidential presentation cut right to the meat and demonstrated the folly of most, cherished, although empty, symbols of governance.

Likely his words were a shock to the ears of board members because it is doubtful if anyone had ever uttered such things aloud before. But careful research and years of working with boards had convinced him that those same concerns were in the minds of many board members, if not yet on their lips.

In developing his model for governance, Carver knew that in spite of the unintentional, though often successful, attempts of boards and their executives to shoot themselves in the foot at the governance level, human reason and logic told them that things were not as they should be. The Policy Governance model he created is a confirmation of that intuitive wisdom, and it challenges the board to step back a few paces from its position and assume a different viewpoint.

In his model, Carver asserts the need for a change of paradigm, or change in the way we have always looked at the board job – and consequently, a different assessment of the individual trustee's responsibility.

Carver writes, "It has been my experience that a simple shift away from detailed and event-specific governance to values and valuing produces a powerful shift in board leadership." (BTMAD p.29)

This *paradigm shift,* as the vernacular has named it, constrains boards to temporarily turn aside from the ways they have traditionally governed, and to consider a different approach. An approach that calls for a facelift of the board's essential role, giving it responsibility – and the procedural wherewithal – for the establishing of *proactive* policies at the utmost levels of governance. Boards will inevitably argue that they already do this; however, a mere cursory reading of their minutes will prove to the contrary.

"School board policymaking as currently construed is a major impediment to leading public education," says Carver (personal paper, A NEW STANDARD OF GOVERNANCE FOR PUBLIC EDUCATION). "Consequently, refocusing boards from administration to policy matters will fail unless the meaning of policy is completely redesigned."

Board members everywhere arrive at the table with the same high dreams and value aspirations. A board that is representative of dedicated people sitting in trusteeship will be receptive to a governance model which shows them how they can be in control instead of in anxiety; how they can be proactive instead of reactive; how they can lead instead of simply trying to stay caught up with the pack.

And how they can be good stewards of their ownership's trust and still have time to be visionary.

The *better way* Carver advocates, is *Policy Governance.*

Of the way today's school boards operate, Mr. W.M. Tierney, a former board trustee had this to say: "If a group of people reasonably familiar with common sense principles of good management sat down to devise an efficient and workable system of governance, the current board design would be the first document they would wad up and toss in the trash can." At the time he made this statement, Tierney had only read of of Dr. Carver's Policy Governance model through literature in the mail. I am convinced it was because of his frustration with past experience that evoked this wisdom into words.

In a conversation I had a few years ago with a very young superintendent, whose anonymity shall be preserved for the sake of the family he supports, he decried that in this high-tech world, he believed the traditional school board was obsolete. I had the impression that the challenge he was encountering with his particular small-town board had driven him to decide it was time to toss the goose out with the sauce.

Fortunately he had not developed sufficient faith in his theory to share it at a board meeting – as I counseled him that public utterance of that notion was tantamount to occupational suicide. There are surely times when administrators might like to throw out the goose with the sauce; but if that goose is the one which lays the golden egg, a gesture of temperance is in order.

But for all its egregious daring, I must say that his claim had some degree of merit: the operative word here being, *traditional.* If the word infers no change – perhaps in decades – in its viewpoints and methods by which the board faces its challenges and connects with its staff and ownership, then in that narrow context of inspection, he was certainly correct.

A board which harbors so constricted a lane for expression that it fosters intellectual sterility is one easily replaced by cardboard cut-outs. And I doubt the group to which he was referring fit that profile.

Boards are ostensibly composed of the wisest and most educated people in the community. And in most minds traditional means something quite different, and not at all disparaging. Boards have a responsibility to uphold the convictions of those who elect them to serve; therefore, they wisely scrutinize any ideological incursion which might bring that trust into jeopardy.

There is a common platitude which says, "If it ain't broke don't fix it," – meaning if things are running smoothly, don't tinker with them. Boards which label themselves as traditional, often subscribe to that old adage, and it is hard to argue that it has not served them well. It does not mean, however, that they are hard-headed or inherently opposed to looking at better ways of doing things. In that broader, more mature context, it is likely that most all boards are traditionalists.

A quote by Tom Peters says, "If it ain't broke, you haven't looked closely enough." The meaning here is crafty, but apparent: In this fast-paced and ever-changing world any systems will be left behind unless its processes are looked at and reconditioned on a regular basis.

Nowhere does that warning resound with greater impact than in the governance process of school boards.

The Indictment of Process

In today's complex educational community, board members find themselves agonizing over the minor details of construction bids, purchasing discounts, clerical and maintenance personnel hiring, building decor and beautification projects. The nearest some school boards actually come to discussing the betterment of children, is to hash out the mundane specifics of student dress code and hair length.

Should school boards have no say in these matters? Certainly they should. However, the *administering* of those matters – important though they are – are areas of *administrative prerogative,* and should be addressed by the board only at the level commensurate with that of its governance position. Governing by policy at the level (and in the manner) Carver suggests would have the board asking itself such questions as, "Why do we want the students to adhere to a dress code in the first place? What are the governing values to be expressed here?"

There are many good reason for codes of student demeanor, of course; but when a board begins to articulate those reasons and extrapolate upward with increasingly higher questions of itself, it can arrive at fascinating value statements about the benefits it desires to bestow upon the child by making its policy decision.

A *value* is an intrinsic principle or quality. As defined by Carver, a value is stated as the driving principle that underpins or supports an action to be taken. It is only sensible then to say that it is the purview and responsibility of the *board* which governs, to define the *values* that govern. But, deciding how best to fulfill the intent of those values is the forte of competent *management.*

Boards, although loathe to admit it, typically turn this arrangement completely around by compelling their administrative staffs to make decisions about volatile matters to be later judged against board values which were yet to be stated.

This *judgment after the fact* was a central theme of George Orwell's **1984**; yet no one challenges the inequality of it in today's public school governance.

To question the integrity of this long-standing philosophy of board process is as challenging as is the acceptance of newer options; but if most boards examine their present *policy* decisions, they will likely find themselves deeply awash in administrative detail that is best left to the school superintendent to decide and perform. The board's immediate response to this charge – by way of question – is, "But how can school superintendents possibly know what we want to do in all these diverse and controversial areas of concern?"

The question is a good one. And the answer is: *they can't, and they don't.*

But the deeper question should be: How can superintendents possibly know what the board wants to do in these areas if it has not first stated the values that govern whatever administrative action should be taken?

Again, with the elementary example of student dress code, if those governing values were first deliberated by the board and then stated in clear, concise policy, the administration could follow those directives in setting workable standards about whatever problems would arise in the area of student behavior in general – without having to run back to the board for its judgment in each and every case.

Hence, Carver's new paradigm of governance – as it draws a hard line in the sand separating administrative management and board governance. Through the creation of specific governance-level policies at the broadest levels, boards are able to give their administrators clear *initiative* guidelines as to what are the expected outputs, and what are the acceptable and/or unacceptable boundaries of application.

These boundaries and limitations, by the way, can be stated in just a few pages of proactive *policy* and almost always concern matters of ethics and prudence.

Boards That Make a Difference was years in the writing, as Carver toiled meticulously to transfer the powerful visual presentation of Policy Governance onto the printed page. The result was, in this author's opinion, the truly definitive bible on the subject of public and nonprofit board governance.

At this time, ***Boards That Make a Difference*** is in its eighth printing and has become the largest seller of its class in its publisher's history. NONPROFIT WORLD referred to it as the most useful full-length book on governing boards to be written in many years.

This book is not intended as a larcenous extraction of John Carver's prestigious work. Such is as unlikely as one author's treatise on New Testament theology being deemed grand theft from St. Paul the Apostle. This is but a small monument erected in admiration.

Carver is the merited authority on governing boards, and his governance model, which this author advocates and teaches, has swept the continent. However, he has written and spoken so extensively on the subject that it would seem an impossible task to appeal for board excellence without having the principles – and indeed many of his personal words – uttered in the same breath. Surely, some of these words are also Carver's – and I strive to give absolute credit where credit is due.

I intend this book for the benefit of trustees and school executives already acquainted with Carver's work as it pertains to nonprofit and public boards in general. Therefore, these pages do not aim at an exhaustive study of the Policy Governance model; rather, they hope to demonstrate some of those concepts beneath examples specific to school boards.

For those who are unfamiliar with Policy Governance, perhaps this cursory palpation of the subject will warrant interest for a more thorough investigation.

Perhaps you will read this book and disagree, and your disagreement is thoroughly appreciated. For without diversity of opinion, perhaps our Western Hemisphere would be stuck with its backside perpetually to the sun. For it is diversity, they say, that makes the world go 'round.

Earlier, I related the conversation with the school superintendent, and I will frequently bring them into focus. However, this book is not specifically about administrators and their staff. Those men and women certainly play vital roles in secondary education, and their contribution and plight will be dealt with in part. But the book is not an assessment of them.

Instead, it is an assessment of their *bosses:* those groups duly elected to govern the school districts which employ these hardworking and dedicated executives. The book is about the group called the *school board.* The discussion will concern itself with an examination of that body as a whole, not with a critique or appraisal of the individual board member.

The reasons for this differentiation are understandable. Individually, board members number in the hundreds of thousands. Perhaps millions. A discussion of the personal values and perspectives of so large a group would likely yield a list too lengthy. It is not inconceivable that a million people could have just as many disparate items on their personal agendas.

But more importantly, since this book will attempt to point out the faults and discrepancies of current board procedures, I make it clear that the charge is not against the people who serve, but against the process. And in this miscarriage of logic and reason, as individuals, board members are not specifically the guilty parties.

If you have ever attended an Edwards Deming seminar, you will have heard one thread pervasive throughout the session: that there is nothing wrong with the American worker or the American work ethic. But, rather, it is the system that is flawed and needs fixing.

The same comment applies to almost all North American public and nonprofit boards – and to school boards particularly: There is nothing wrong with the individual board member or his or her ethic. The flaws of board governance lie in the system itself.

Professionals who work before boards on a regular basis quickly come to stand in awe at the selfless commitment shown by these volunteer servants. The paradox created by their sometimes awkward predicament is not unlike a sport's team roster composed of world-class athletes competing on the field with an ill-conceived game plan. It would be as harshly unjustified to blame school board members for the dysfunctional processes they have inherited from precedent boards as it would be to hold culpable the eldest son for the sins of the father.

Let me add that as I questioned my anonymous superintendent further, he readily retreated from his foolhardy proposal and agreed with my own more qualified disclaimer. That it is the current inadequate design of the board job that puts the integrity and workability of boards at risk.

Far from being obsolete, the school board is an institution whose capacity for vision and leadership pleads for – and is ready for – the genesis of rebirth.

"But such a rebirth of board leadership will not arise from adjustments made to an inadequate model," says, Carver, "no matter how time-honored and comfortably familiar its methods. The conventional wisdom and the existing model of school governance is not up to the task."

People who sit on boards work very hard. The undeniable requirement for excellence is that they must now learn to work smarter.

Before moving on to the next chapter, I reiterate that the book is not meant as a condemnation of people, but of a process flawed. Not of individuals, but of an archaic governance design that is of necessity exercised by boards whose obsession should be the constant creation and recreation of organizational vision and excellence.

The governance concepts expressed here represent an indelible outline toward a new – more sensible – way of specifying and fulfilling the board's responsibility to the school district it *sits atop*. And for one to say that the governing board *sits atop* the district is not a hyperbolic compliment; as, indeed, most boards see themselves as the *Final Authority*.

What could *possibly* be higher than that?

CHAPTER TWO

THE BOARD MUST BE IN CONTROL

Whatever redesign may be in order for the framework of today's school board governance, several possibilities for compromise should be carefully guarded against. First, this change does not, in itself, call for replacement of those sitting on the board, for they are the ones who possess the greatest opportunity for achieving this move toward excellence. Second, any shift in governing style must improve, rather than diminish the board's integrity as trustee owner of the district.

Until now the design theory to accomplish so delicate an undertaking has long remained hidden in the crevices and mossy rocks of tradition.

One has only to casually browse the mall bookstore to confirm the proliferation of literature available on the subject of management. Shelf upon shelf is replete with information applicable to every facet of managerial endeavors — business, staff, financial, etc. Yet finding material pertinent to the *governance* process of the board is an exercise in futility.

As management techniques have acquired greater sophistication — particularly since the end of the 1960's — knowledge acquisition in the specialized field of *governance* has remained virtually static. Every school administrator worth his or her salt has a personal library of this accumulation of management knowledge — some so extensive that the trunks of their cars would not hold it. Yet how many of us who sit on boards can boast of reading more than one or two books specifically about the field of *governance*?

John Carver discovered this inequity when he first began searching for light on the subject; and he charitably refers to it as a gap created between the sophistication of management and the sophistication of the board (BTMAD p.24). On an eye-to-eye level it might be compared to the ever-widening gulf between the computer-literate generation of today and we elders who doggedly endure with card files and ledger sheets. (If it were not for the insistence of my own son, the engineer, I might be preserving these scribblings with a Bic pen and a yellow tablet.)

Yet our human desire to serve – and our dedication to that task – constrain boards to persevere. Perhaps only an austere philosophy of optimism on our part as trustees, often born out of sheer confidence in the institutions we govern, and the value of that same institutional legacy, has underwritten the board's influence throughout this management renaissance.

But can this *societal sponsorship* of a leadership body falling so far behind its own legions be long sustained?

Boards have been in existence for millennia, and those who serve are elite among peers, placed in positions of trust with devout community attention and participation. Their systems for governing have coexisted throughout those same eons; but the time has come to breathe in new life and bring boards on par with those management professionals who stand in line behind them.

Only the board, itself, can do this. No other entity can impose it. It must begin by self-evaluation of board processes – of its strengths, its weaknesses, its needs...and its naivete.

As trustees will point out, State statutes say the school board is responsible for governing and managing the school district. And although it does not take a Supreme Court Justice to see that being responsible for managing and actually doing the managing is not the same thing, many boards try very hard to do it, anyway.

This, in spite of the fact that we call ourselves the board of governors and not the board of managers.

The board is no more capable nor expected to personally manage the district than it is expected to personally prepare a budget; issue bonds; or hire teachers. However, since the board is held accountable for the moral and fiscal goings-on of the district, what excuse can there be for it not being in control?

There is none. Yet this necessity for our boards to be firmly at the helm, and our near absolute inability to achieve it – coupled with the inherited deficiencies that have been handed down from ancestral boards – all combine to place us precipitously close to zero workability.

What is Control?

Control, in the minds of some people, means having hands-on command of everything that takes place. If nothing else, fear that we are not in control drives us toward that fulfillment. Television and movies conjure up panicked politicians scurrying about making life miserable for those unfortunate enough to be their subordinates. In my brief experience I have not seen this from boards; for who among us will not admit that this kind of control is an impossibility? Not even the superintendent can guarantee that tight of rein; and he or she is on site eight hours a day, five days a week. What can a part-time group with no specific expertise in the day-to-day management of a school district hope to accomplish? It has neither the time nor skill to control every action of its staff.

However, contends Carver, by the utilization of a value-specific governance model the board does not have to. For with this type of model, such an inexpert group of above average intelligent people can not only obtain clear accountability, but in the process, can gain the expert capacity to *lead.*

Admittedly, lacking the formula for this dubious magic potion, the clearest route has been one of tight oversight —unfortunately often bordering on and drifting into the quagmire of micromanagement. What the board really needs for leadership control is not *control-for-control's-sake*, but simply a method of exercising due care and responsibility in governing the district, and being able to clearly demonstrate that integrity upon demand. In the eyes of the rational, that achievement alone would allow us a clear conscience by day and a good sound sleep by night.

Having said all that, the reality still exists that State law makes the board accountable for everything that goes on; and that can certainly be scary. In a school district which monthly disseminates millions of dollars, the fear that even a few of those might turn up in question on the Six-O'clock Watchdog News Hour is enough to drive members to drastic steps of control.

More than one member has asked aloud why a body

that is held accountable for so much is allotted so little time each month to meet and isn't even given on-site offices from which its trustees can supervise. It doesn't seem a fair arrangement, does it?

Occasionally I overhear a board member remark, "The public doesn't realize it, but this could be a full-time job." When I hear that, I understand their need to feel as involved in the process as possible. However, one only has to attend an open-to-the-public forum to discover that the trustee had it all wrong. For sadly, the public does think that the board's job is a full-time job. For that reason unrealistic public demands are made of board members, against which no one has yet gained political courage to rise and question the impracticality.

Mr. Kenneth Graeber, board trustee with Tomball Independent School District told me his wife had recently asked him about a menial matter which had taken place the day before on one of the school campuses. When he told her he had not heard about it, she was shocked.

"You mean you're on the board and you don't know about that?" She said.

He said it pointed out the true extent of the problem. If his wife presumes he should be infinitely familiar with every little thing that takes place throughout the district, how can the public expect less?

Yet, when a trustee says that the board job could be full-time, the comment has a richer content because many times it is an indication that the trustee concurs with that notion and is involving himself too much in administrative matters.

This is not to mean the board should be unconcerned or have no say-so in the way the district's business is conducted, but it does speak to the ways we go at trying to achieve responsible oversight. By trying to minutely control the myriad systems operating daily in the administrative process – personnel, purchasing, financial management, asset protection, etc. – we delude ourselves into assuming we can secure better control.

This undertaking is as futile as were I to attempt personal control of each automotive system operating beneath the hood of my car – electrical, lubrication, hydraulics, fuel injection, and air conditioning, for example.

The new Lexus boasts of ninety-plus separate systems – all controlled by a central computerized master. If I tried to personally control all this complex, internal gadgetry, the car might run – although I doubt smoothly. However, even if it did, it would not be going anywhere because the driver would now have become just another part of the system. Who would sit up front to govern? Who could even see the road ahead?

It may sound flippant, but I much prefer the way my auto manufacturer designed the car. He wisely put me in the driver's seat with the proper mechanisms within reach for me to govern the car, and he designed a master control system to ensure proper operation of the sub-systems beneath the hood.

I sit up front with the steering wheel, the foot pedals and a clear view of the road ahead. I have reliable instruments in front of me, whereby I can efficiently *monitor* how things are going outside my personal control. The digital read-outs tell me at a glance if something is amiss – leaving me free to govern the car to whatever destination I desire.

The Futility of Control

I recently learned of a school board that had gone into executive session and returned to announce it had fired its superintendent because of *"differences in educational ideology"* and had seized control of administration. The only reason I can envision for a school board having to seize control is if it were not in control to begin with. Yet, if we had polled members of the board prior to its decision to terminate the administrator, likely each would have said it was in control.

They would have told us that they interacted regularly with staff in seeing that all programs and projects were correctly administered. They might have said the board had personally cooperated in devising the means of achieving certain goals; and that it demanded all staff-initiated documents be brought to the board for approval before action could be taken.

One wonders how a board so involved in controlling had taken so long in discovering the "ideological differences", and should have had to seize control.

In truth, this board was very busy controlling; but it was *not in control.*

My neighbor once bought a new car with a diesel engine. It was a beautiful car, and for the first few days he seemed very satisfied, although he said it did not have much "get-up-and-go." Being a shade-tree mechanic, he decided to remedy the situation by taking it inside his garage and *adjusting* the systems.

As the car's acceleration went from bad to worse, so also did his tinkering – as his growing dissatisfaction took him beneath the hood time and again. Eventually he became so displeased that he took the car back to the dealer and demanded action. They made him a fair deal on another one and he traded.

As with the school district situation, there was nothing wrong with the vehicle. More likely it just had a bad case of *tinkeritis*. And similarly, as with the school board, my neighbor had now *seized* control of the situation – and fired his car.

Unless he and the board had gained insight from these incidents, they are apt to be repeated over and again. My neighbor will someday inform me that this new car – having been mechanically altered into jalopydom – was traded in for another; and the school board will announce that its superintendent was later dismissed because of "a difference in educational philosophy" and the board has once again *seized control.*

In the overwhelming number of cases, boards' attempts at this control is entirely benevolent, since a board that is not firmly at the helm of command is not demonstrating competence in the realm of moral and legal accountability. The moral part, many members can live with; but the legal part is a different slice of the pie altogether.

Far from suffering some insatiable Czar or Czarina complex, trustees are simply reacting to the owner/taxpayer demand that they be good stewards of the public purse. Given the absence of an acceptable governance model to provide a viable alternative, the board has chosen the only other sensible course. Yet, if the circle remains unbroken it is likely to happen again, and the board will still not be in control.

Carver continually points out the weakness of the board's *reactive stance,* reacting to staff initiatives rather than taking the initiative. What could more clearly demonstrate reactivity in a board's bearing than having to take extreme steps after-the fact in order to establish its control.

One board trustee talked to me about this and quipped, "I guess that's why we make the big bucks."

So, we ask, what's a board to do?

If staying on top of ongoing administrative programs and projects, *and listening* to and reading an endless parade of staff reports is not exhibiting control of the district, then what is it?

If demonstrating our governance accountability through the tight prescription of administrative means is no guarantee of board control, then what is it?

If requiring our official board stamp of approval of all projected staff initiatives, budgetary and purchasing documents is not showing good stewardship of the public purse, then what is it?

If rehashing, reviewing and redoing much of what our staff has already done so we can be assured of competent awareness is not an illustration of responsible leadership, then what is it?

Well, inclusively *it* is a lot of well-intended things; but it is *not good governance.*

The board must be a well-informed board, but its greatest need is to be informed about the right things. When boards assess the problem of control in this light, it becomes synonymous with having dependable information and the assurance of acceptable administrative means leading to acceptable ends.

The hitch comes in achieving this goal without being intrusive, and without impeding the district's momentum through the tight bottleneck at the board-approval level.

Is this possible?

It may sound like an ambitious claim – made this early in the text – but I expect to show how Policy Governance outlines ways for the board to more efficiently connect with its administrator and set expectations; to safely monitor all systems beyond its personal control; and thereby to be able to work *on the system* without having to work *in the system.*

CHAPTER THREE

THE CONTROL MIRAGE

Control, like the illusive quality of beauty, is in the eye of the beholder. A friend of mine who had been blinded by an accident when he was in his late teens asked me if his wife was pretty. He had met and married her years after losing his sight, and apparently was just now coming around to wondering what she looked like. The woman was a petite blond with a very pleasing face, and I told him I thought she was pretty. He said he didn't think so.

What obscure standard was he using to make this judgment?

In most cases, the areas of concern over which boards wish to exercise control are legitimate; but the methods they employ to obtain this control and the standards used to judge its success are as deceptive as those used by my blind friend to assess his wife's appearance.

Regardless of the effort made or the method used, the outcome is sure to yield one thing above all else. That one thing is a complaint by staff – more covert than open – that the board is meddling in places where it has no business by intruding in the workplace.

Intrusion and The Siren's Song of Connecting

Do we, as school board trustees have the right to intrude in the management methods and application of administration? Certainly we do. Particularly since the law says the board has the legal power and duty to manage and govern the district? The board sits in trusteeship for the true owners, which are the taxpayers. As does any owner of a business, it has the right to do whatever it wishes – within the moral and legal restraints of its statutes. In fact, the board has greater latitude for action than do the real owners, themselves; because by electing the board and seating it in its stead, the public has duly delegated that authority.

State law also specifically says that individual members shall not exercise authority over the district, its property or its employees. This is a necessary and well-intended statute; however, without further internal policy on the board's part, it opens the door to intrusion by giving members the right to *"seek information from district records and employees".*

That right should not be taken from the board, nor even limited – except in ways that it might protect the board from itself. Certainly, having clear access to "right-to-know" information is paramount to ownership. But when that free access tempts the board deeper into administrative trivia rather than cementing its position as governor, the result can be debilitating. For a board that intrudes in the trenches of administration cannot see over the tall heads of its troops.

The board is, therefore, encouraged to rechannel its full influence through proactive policies and to elevate itself to a much higher rampart for viewing the horizon.

"Intrusion" is a word we understand; but intrusion can lead to "meddling" – a word whose exact meaning we haven't had agreement on. In this use, *meddling* is defined as prescribing or setting out the means or circumstances the board wants its staff involved in. This is a violation of good governance and of good management as well. Deciding administrative means should be a function of management.

"The staff needs freedom from the board's friendly intrusion to do its work." writes Carver (BTMAD, p. 108).
"The board cheats the mission by constraining too much;
it risks cheating standards of acceptable conduct by constraining too little. Proactively setting relatively few limits for the CEO increases the freedom of both the board
and the CEO."

A further definition of meddling will be brought out
later; but for the discussion of control, it suffices to say
that simply keeping up with what's going on cannot in
itself be meddling.

Do you recall your first day on the board? Your first
meeting? Do you remember the sudden realization that
there was much more going on there than you had realized? Did you wonder how in the world you would be
able to learn about it all – much less be able to keep up?
You may have even questioned your decision to get on
the board in the first place – fearing that you had bitten
off more than you could chew.

In talking with former and current board trustees, I
find these feelings to be the norm. And when it occurs,
the human reaction is to quickly look around for a sturdy
handle by which we can achieve some measure of control
and accountability. After all, each of us brings some kind
of occupational expertise to the board; so it is only natural that we turn our faces toward that same area of the
organization. If we can connect to the day-to-day affairs
of administration in our particular field of knowledge and
interest, we can become informed and thereby achieve control
in that small area – if nowhere else.

This compartmentalized connecting, as the board for-
ages about trying to find its handle on control, is most

noticeable in the areas of administration that are most visible, such as budgeting, purchasing, construction, etc.

If you will excuse the jocular latitude I have granted myself, let's run through a few worse case scenarios and see whom we turn up in these tempting areas for meddling. It is quite possible that we might recognize someone – other than ourselves—with whom we have served at one time or another.

The Budget

Sarah is a new trustee, and in her professional life, an efficient and fiscally conservative CPA. She realizes many of the things being discussed at the first meeting are important; however, experience has taught her that money is where the real control lies. She feels if she can just get a good handle on the budget, she can see to it that the district is properly steered in the right direction. Keeping up with the budget is where she feels comfortable and in control; and last month's financial statement always requires her detailed scrutiny before the board gets her nod of approval.

But alas, the budget is a chimerical administrative tool, not a steering device. Attempting to control the organization by means of a document that is likely out-of-balance the very next day of its life is as futile as finding the good fishing place by the mark you made last week on the side of the boat.

The same is even more apparent for last month's financial statement. Steering the district by a document that is admittedly out-of-date is not unlike driving a car by watching the scenery disappearing behind you. When the board gets her nod and they all raise their hands to approve it, what are they approving? That last month existed?

Can anyone recall the last time the previous month's financial statement was not approved?

Personnel

George is also a new trustee who manages a large janitorial service for a living. He has been in business a long time and knows the value of having good people working for you. In his years he has developed his own psychology for getting the most from employees and now sees how he can pass that valuable knowledge along to the district.

"People is where the power is," he says; so a taut bridle on personnel policies and hiring practices is the thing the board should do. The other board members know of George's success in town and readily accept him as the board's conscience on matters of district personnel. It is alleged that George can simply look at a teacher and tell if she's capable of controlling a class of unruly students. When time comes for the current personnel committee chairperson to step down, George will get the job.

Money and people are the two things boards worry about most because those are the two areas that, if neglected, can easily get them into trouble. School boards have legitimate concerns about personnel being mistreated. There are concerns that legal problems may occur because of no clear grievance path to the board. They worry that staff might be underpaid, thereby losing valuable experience to the private sector. They worry that staff is overpaid, which might get them in political trouble with the district.

George and Sarah are dedicated professionals who display exemplary efficiency and responsibility in their chosen fields. But, as board trustees, they are perhaps acting irresponsibly.

A Canadian board insisted on having the board president and the chairman of the personnel committee advise the executive in hiring the administrative assistant. Its rationale was that if the board takes a personal hand in choosing the employee to fill the position, it would have more interest in seeing to it that the person "made the grade".

I pointed out that, admirable though it was, it is not the board's place to nurture staff through the work process. Choosing staff assistants is a task of administration. If the executive opts for a style of nurturing so that staff members "make the grade", that is the administrator's choice.

Besides, when one's boss sits down at one's side to advise, does one really take it only as advice? In some jurisdictions, school boards immerse themselves in the hiring of teachers by "advising" the administrator. How often does an administrator turn thumbs down on the board's advice?

Diet

Lucille raised three sons and two daughters, all of them growing into tall and healthy adults. Don't try to feed her any of this "phony baloney" modern diet stuff. She knows what kind of food "sticks to a kid's ribs". Every Monday morning finds the kitchen staff getting briefed on what Lucille wants done during the week. Following that will be a detailed report to her on how much food was left on the trays last week.

Lucille is a great mother and nurturer of children. But as a board trustee she is missing her greater calling.

Purchasing

Ralph and DeeDee are veteran trustees. Before retiring, Ralph ran a tire store; and DeeDee's husband owns a construction business specializing in interstate highway bridges. Control is synonymous with purchasing, they say, because nothing happens until money is spent. Hence, the review of bids and control of bid policy becomes their bailiwick.

Since coming on the board two years earlier, Ralph has extended his expertise far beyond mere wheels and tires. He now knows everything there is to know about batteries, about heavy-duty lawn mowers, and even about the high-tech equipment in the kitchen. DeeDee is equally knowledgeable in the area of construction bids – with the letting of small jobs to local contractors being her specialty.

Both these trustees are a tribute to the dedication citizens have to serve on school boards; and it is common to find them deeply involved in the construction *specs* of everything from built-up asphalt roofs on out-buildings to sidewalks and jogging trails on campus.

Yet, they, like their colleagues George, Lucille and Sarah—while doing things that are well-intended – are contributing not only to poor governance, but to poor management as well.

There are many legitimate reasons for boards to have anxiety in these important areas, so attempting close control at the hands-on level is understandable. But the counterproductivity generated by these methods may far outweigh the advantages gained. For one has to ask, why does this school district need a superintendent? What is there for him to do?

In these examples where the board feels it is merely

exercising its position as trustee to show responsibility in these legitimate areas of concern, we find an elected body with seven sets of arms, grasping at an undetermined number of straws.

Rather than dictating the means and requiring detailed verification of the way school district business is carried forth, the board should undergo an up-front, inner examination and ask itself something that has not even been mentioned:

What are the educational values that we want fulfilled by the district? What are the attitudes and understandings we want the children to acquire from the school system? And in the fulfillment of those values, what kinds of actions by the administration would the board find unacceptable? (In the enigmatic paradox that is fiscal accountability, it is always the unacceptable rather than the acceptable, that causes the most concern. So, why not center our governance attention on that?).

This perspective does not imply that the board should be uninvolved, or even *less involved.* A board should bring as much leadership through involvement as possible. But, as with the need to be informed, the board should be involved in the right things. That right thing should be a continuing dialogue about the education of children and not the construction and maintenance of the district's real and personal property.

In such a hierarchical society as that existing in the board/staff relationship, the counterproductive aspects of this kind of board involvement can be humorously compared to the act of a playful toddler dashing across the lawn to interact with a flock of foraging sparrows. For with intrusion lurks the inevitable threat of inviting the board to become more deeply involved in the details of administration. And hence, as defined above, the irresistible temptation to meddle.

Still, the need to connect is a common lure which some boards handle by a more hands-off approach, opting for getting the relevant facts through monthly reports – either having them sent to the trustees' homes or presented at the meeting.

Administrative staffs, therefore, regularly spend uncounted costly hours preparing project reports so that the board can be kept abreast of what is going on. These projects are almost always staff initiated, and many depend upon the board's verbal approval before they can be moved forward to the next level. But can the board really be brought well enough up to speed in the short span of a board meeting for it to make informed approval decisions when large amounts of money are at stake?

Doubtful. Yet thousands of dollars in staff time are spent in the generation and presentation of these reports for the board's assimilation.

Dr. Gregory Bogard is a former school board president and has this to say in a personal communication, "Many trustees do not even read the board material that is mailed to them until they get to the meetings. They do their cramming after they get there, and waste the time of the administration while they try to get up to speed on whatever issues they must vote on."

This common allegation is not difficult to confirm; however, here again, the fault lies with the system and not entirely with the malfeasant trustee. It is necessary for board members to have material sent to their homes, for it is the most logical procedure. But what is it they are being sent?

School boards are as susceptible as any nonprofit or public board to the beguiling discussion of trivia. The board job is a talking job – it does not teach geometry, coach football, or cut the grass. Carver contends that of all the pitfalls lying in wait for boards, the *Trivia Trap* is the one most often fallen into; and a board will discuss just about anything that is raised – often lifting the handling of trivia to an art form.

It sounds redundant, but likely most literature sent to board members involves matters of administration which could have been dealt with (by staff) through proactive guideline policies.

If the board were deliberating at a higher level, the stack would be shorter, the details less menial, and the implications of board decisions would be more dramatic. And, certainly, the amount of staff time spent in preparation would be down-sized.

As board members, we have a right to be kept informed on a timely basis about anything we need – and want – to know; and staffs have an obligation to make it so. In fact, Policy Governance dictates specifically that such a requirement be spelled out in the board's policies. No one is saying the board has no right to stay caught up on *everything* if it wishes.

"Just keeping up with a large staff can take prodigious hours and even then can never be done fully." (Carver, BTMAD, p.11). He has often said that, even if the board could somehow keep up with everything that was going on in administration, "There isn't an ounce of leadership in keeping up."

Imagine two people in a foot race. One is ahead, and the other one is keeping up. Which would you say is the leader?

Control Through Approval

Simon Says Stop - Simon Says Go

The board meeting minutes from a $60 million district showed it consuming precious time debating whether staff could spend $20 thousand for a copier/duplicator. The motion passed by a full show of hands and was followed by a similar vote to amend the budget. Was the school board acting irresponsibly in bothering with this means issue? The answer is a qualified Yes. Without a functionable model to help it separate its job from that of staff, it was doing what seemed the responsible thing to do.

I ask, what was the board's governing policy on matters such as this? Must the administrator of so large an organization come for board approval on all matters of this significance? Is the administrator incapable of deciding this issue?

Boards have the responsibility for deciding the parameters within which purchases should be made by administration – to achieve specified results, and within a stipulated reasonable cost. Considering the figure of which this district's budget boasts, is this not a trivial amount for a governing body to concern itself with? If state law requires close oversight of purchases in this range, could not a proactive limitations policy *govern* authority to the administrator with the board's assent coming on consent agenda? Under this arrangement, would not the board be able to defend whatever decision the superintendent made?

When boards make it their business to prescribe the means – and therefore, the means material – as this board had done, the door swings open for individual trustees to bring their own list of things administration should purchase for the district.

Another large district wasted valuable governing time going over a "comparison study" as to whether administration should use artificial potted plants in its offices or the real thing. In the end, one particular trustee insisted on fingering through the document line by line, demanding that staff provide detailed explanation of each index.

This "Simon Says" mentality, where administration must run to the board for approval of every type administrative move imaginable, is the thinking style that keeps boards penned down to mediocrity like Caesar's Legion under siege. If the board is worried that its concerned publics might object to the district spending money on flowers – either natural or otherwise – why not simply express that particular value issue in an up-front policy of executive limitation?

Even if frivolous administrative overspending were the fear, through the integrity of Policy Governance, the board can safely specify the prudence and ethics values that would securely govern that area. With proper policy in place at the board level to spell out the initiative guidelines, this kind of administrative matter would not have required the taking of valuable board time.

The Control Charade

Administrators, by being the board's willing accomplices in many of these charades, are not without their own benefaction.

"When I was on the board," says Dr. Bogard, "I was reminded of parents hiding Easter eggs and then leading the little ones around close enough to find the hidden eggs. The school administration hides the eggs and endures board meetings long enough for the trustees to find them."

As board members, we like to boast that we are the final authority, and that we are in control of the district. Yet who is it that tells us what we must talk about at each meeting?

State law says that it is the duty of the superintendent to prepare board agendas *in cooperation with the board president* (my emphasis). But isn't it true that on the morning of the monthly meeting, the board president will call the superintendent and say, "Well, what's on the agenda for tonight?"

If your board is that one in a *zillion* that prepares its own agenda, then I laud you. But when a board takes the initiative and decides what it will talk about, what does it have to say? Does it talk about the wallpaper bids for the Home Economics Cottage? Should the Ag Department buy a Chevy van or a Ford? How much should we pay our secretaries? What about staff group insurance? Should the bus barn get a tin roof or fiberglass?Do we want to use AT&T or two tin cans and a string? Uh-oh—sorry, we've run out of time.

For the majority of boards – too large a number to christen— the staff decides, and therefore, "governs" what the board talks about; and the discussion at the table often goes about as I have drawn. Perhaps at the next meeting there will be an opportunity to discuss strategic leadership and the education of children.

If the board agenda is decided by staff prerogative, then who is really exercising control? Staffs quickly learn how to play dodge ball with the board and give it what it wants; for, it's pretty easy to have all the right answers if one knows in advance what the questions are.

Does anyone believe that a seasoned administrator will

risk disaster for one of his programs by placing it on the agenda before being sure it will pass muster? If the superintendent's values are not well-intended, will a cursory perusal of a "stacked" document by a school board on a tight agenda be sufficient to protect owner interests?

The potential for this anomaly came to me from a discussion I attended with the superintendent of an Atlantic Coast State. During the taped conversation he made the statement, "In the limited time the board has, it can't possibly become knowledgeable about all the programs we have going. We use this to our advantage in accomplishing what we feel the district needs."

As I frantically fumbled for the Off button on the recorder, he added flatly, "We use them."

Then he noticed my panic and smiled. "Don't worry," he said. "They know it. They condone it. It's an unspoken but understood agreement."

I asked him why; and he said it made both their jobs a lot easier. "The board trusts me to do the right thing."

This borders on Carver's description of what he calls a *cheerleader board.* "The hallmark is trust and loose control," says Carver, in demurely recounting the board's SOP rationale.

Cheerleader boards see themselves as lofty volunteers working *for* a capable CEO whom they can trust and confidently support. Administration even at its topmost pertinence is no concern of theirs, they feel; and they display their confidence and appreciation for a job well-done by use of the symbolic ink pad and rubber stamp of approval.

In my household I use a similar approach.

"I'm the husband," I say to my wife. "So, I should sign off on the big decisions."

No problem. She makes the big decisions and lets me

approve when I get home. If it's something I really should decide, she presents the choices – usually two. I can either choose one or the other, and she always leads me to the one which is right. As with the school board Dr. Bogard mentioned above, she hides the eggs and I pretend not to notice when she hints where they are.

It makes both our jobs easier, also.

It may sound like an over-simplification, but the variance on this theme swings the spectrum. School boards which fall victim to this *rubber-stamp syndrome* clearly present their executives with the temptation to become manipulator.

These are classic examples of what John Carver has said countless times: Boards pretend to govern; and staffs pretend to work for them.

In closing this chapter, I quote a former administrator now retired and serving as school board president:

"A school board that is attempting to control by prescribing how its manager should manage, has exchanged its part-time governance job with full-time potential, for a part-time management job with full-time mediocrity.

"Let's say you're the owner of a multi-million dollar company, and ask yourself if you would connect with a staff of managers in the manner by which school boards try to exercise control over the district. The corporate board is hardly an exemplary model, but if the primitive governance processes of school boards were examined beneath the harsh daylight of logic, someone with wisdom would quickly push back from the table and draw the blinds."

CHAPTER FOUR

DEFICIENCIES OF THE SYSTEM

As a Tree Withers From the Root

In personal correspondence from Dr. Arzell L. Ball, former Superintendent now retired, of Richardson Independent School District in Richardson, Texas, he mentioned the tenuous balance of power between board and administration and the short tenure of the typical school superintendent, as being some of the tough issues facing school districts in the 1990's. Of course, it is easy to say there is a shortage of good superintendent material – and it may be true. I, as grandparent, am strangely more particular about those qualities than twenty years ago when I did not have this esteemed position. Cerainly not every man or woman can be Superintendent of Schools, as is not everyone qualified to sit on a school board. But, as I pointed out earlier, probably many reasons for short tenure of superintendents lie not with failure of the people involved – whether they be management or board. Instead, they stem from the flawed process which governs both.

Let me return to my conversation with the anonymous school superintendent that I mentioned in the first chapter. He will remain anonymous, so I will call him *Raymond Doe*. In spite of his gruesome suggestion, Raymond was in a lively mood. "I'm between periods of unemployment," he said.

At first I thought he had meant to say "between periods of *EMployment*". Perhaps he had lost his job and was using comic relief to tell me he was temporarily out of work. But, no, he had said it the way he intended. He had just recently acquired a new superintendent's position with a nice rural district not too far from his wife's home town.

"It's a great opportunity," he said. "But if experience is any teacher at all, it'll come to an end soon enough."

You see, he had been using comic relief all right; but to hint that he felt sure the job wouldn't last – to infer that although working in an excellent position, for the time being he was in fact just between periods of UNemployment.

This was Raymond's third placement in nine years. His first job had lasted five, and the second one was for four. In his state, the average time for a superintendent to remain in one place is four years. So, he had covered the point spread and held onto his job long enough to freeze the odds.

I knew him to be an honest administrator and a man dedicated to excellence in public education. Furthermore, I knew by reputation that the school district from which he had just come was one which shared that same dedication. My incredulity that this seemingly perfect match had ended so abruptly prompted me to ask the obvious, "What happened?"

"The people on that board were just impossible to work with," he said. "It wasn't my fault."

Oh, sure, I said to myself. It's never our fault, is it? It's always *them* who's to blame. But, what was behind the breaking up of this *marriage made in heaven* lay deeper in the rest of Raymond's accounting.

"I never could figure out what they wanted me to do. If I moved in the direction I thought they wanted me to go, they would come back and say it was the wrong direction. If I moved left, they wanted me to the right. If I moved right, they wanted me to the left. Toward the end, I had no idea what they wanted, and sometimes they changed their minds in mid-stream."

I asked him if the board indicated that it wanted some kind of futuristic shift of priorities or something?

"No, and I never proposed anything draconian, if that's what you mean. In fact, their strategic plan for the district looked about like it looks today. I felt like I was in a time loop."

"Well, surely you kept the board abreast of things going on, didn't you?"

"Constantly. In fact, they wanted regular reports on everything we did. That's one of the ways I'd find out we were headed in the wrong direction."

I asked, "Were the trustees much in agreement on things?"

"Yes. They saw to it that there was no controversy. If controversy arose, they would just put it aside for another time and never come back to it."

This wasn't my first conversation of this type, and I was starting to see a pattern. No futuristic demands, no controversy. What could have gone wrong?

"I tell you, it just amazes me," he said. "For three years I was in agreement with them, and I thought they agreed with the direction I was taking the district."

"What's so amazing about that?"

"Well, I'm amazed that it took me another year to figure out it was the wrong direction."

"That last year must have been a joy," I said.

He didn't answer. I could tell he was thinking. "They had an election that year," he mused. "Maybe it was the new members."

Maybe so. But maybe not.

The school board Raymond described was a selfless group of public servants, struggling to fulfill a role as trustee owner of the district and to answer its calling with as much discretion as mature adults can bring to a task. The hard-working group he described could easily have been a board in almost any part of America.

School boards are under tremendous pressure to produce. Individual parents and parent groups, public and private advocacy groups – any or all of which might rightfully show up at a board meeting demanding action of one sort or another. These owners, perhaps each armed with their own burning agenda and idea of what should be achieved – and therefore what action should be taken – present formidable opponents for debate. Add to that a news media seemingly waiting for controversy to arise, and a determination to succeed is generated that exceeds even what the trustees, themselves, believed they were capable of.

Yet the board trustee role is so vaguely defined and so misguided by the whims of community tradition, that the success achieved, and the victory spoils obtained by that success are sometimes impossible to demonstrate and measure. The visual translation of that hoped-for success is so cloudy that few boards can even describe what it is – either before forehand or after.

So, we ask the question, how can school boards know when they are successful if they have not been able to define what that success is to be?

In **Boards That Make a Difference**, John Carver issued a list of board flaws (p.10-11), some of which have been mentioned in this text. These flaws, or board-system deficiencies cannot help but spawn poor governance. In making his list, Carver was gracious in pointing out that "Although some boards may avoid a few...rarely does any one board avoid them all."

Likewise some school boards, by having been blessed with powerful internal leadership and efficient administrative staffs, are able to elude many of the maladies with which Raymond's former board was struggling.

Let's examine his comments and see what those maladies were. He said that nothing he initiated seemed to satisfy the board, and that he couldn't figure out what they wanted him to do. "...and sometimes they changed their minds in mid-stream."

A Message in the Sand

Absence of Clear Instructions

It is not uncommon to witness a staff struggling to flesh out what seemed to be the board's majority opinion expressed at the last meeting. This is almost a universal complaint by superintendents, as boards commonly leave their administrators in the dark about what is expected of them.

Boards, however, will argue they do no such thing – and can say so with serious conviction, because each member has a vivid recollection of the item in question.

"I'm sure we went over that in the last meeting. I recall specifically when so-and-so brought it up, and we all agreed it was a good thing."

So, there you have it. So-and-so brought it up, others agreed, and from that the staff is supposed to deduce that the order to act had been given. The opportunity for trouble knocks even harder when staff has listened to the discussion and taken the bait. Mr. so-and-so said it, the majority of the board seemed to agree, and the school superintendent took action on it.

Between this meeting and the next Mr. so-and-so's great

idea may lose support around the table, and, to quote Raymond, "They seemed to change their minds in mid-stream".

Items that are discussed but not committed to written policy have a way of falling from grace and disappearing from the agenda. Raymond indicated he frequently didn't know what the board wanted and found himself out on a limb because they had moved in a certain direction that had not been officially stated. Often the board's commentary on that comes after the initiative has been taken and turns out to be wrong for some reason the board never bothered to define in the beginning.

Veteran school administrators have learned early in their careers that acting on what seems to be the loudest opinion at a board meeting is as risky as buying a Rolex from a street vendor.

As consultants, we can say these things; however, as board members we will rightfully argue that the practice of committing every instruction to the superintendent in writing would be too bulky and time consuming.

"It would take us forever and a day to get through a meeting," one trustee might say. "If we had to constantly instruct the superintendent in writing, there wouldn't be any time left for tackling the important issues."

This trustee's point is well taken. And Policy Governance is certainly not what that is about. In fact, just the opposite.

Policy Governance is about dealing with the board's job in such a way so that constant instructions are not needed.

If that seems strange, then you read it correctly.

Let's examine more of Raymond's conversation.

The Forked Tongue Syndrome

Absence of Single Voice

Carver uses the term, "The board speaks with one voice, or not at all."

In speaking of his board, Raymond used the word *they* eleven times, and the words *them* and *their* once each. Never once did he refer to the board in the singular. Always in the plural.

It was obvious that Raymond considered the board to be an assembly of different voices and opinions – not one body. Of course, the board is a group of people with varying opinions and often polarized agendas. It would not surprise me to learn that he was hearing from – and being given orders by – every individual member on the board. Little wonder that he couldn't figure out what *they* wanted him to do.

No one would argue that this is not an acceptable way to manage things, i.e., giving one man seven bosses at once. Yet, seldom does someone on a board raise the point to consider that it just might not be too good a way to govern things, either.

Consider my own case. I have two daughters, and five granddaughters. If each of them at once were demanding something different from me, I can imagine looking like a distressed octopus taken captive by the Seven Dwarfs. Fortunately I can throw my hands into the air and stomp angrily from the house. But staff cannot do that – and is left to search about for some viable path, that hopefully is acceptable to the board's majority opinion or loudest voice.

The board members' response to this is that the reason they are on the board in the first place is to give input to staff and to direct it to fulfill that trustee's sworn promise to his or her constituency. For surely, if during the campaign, a school board candidate pledged to do something about hot lunches, for example, or efficient transportation, then shouldn't their position on the board be directed toward keeping that promise?

The answer is, yes it should. However, it should be done at the level of governance, not the level of administration. Board members are governors, not managers of staff activities.

The Road to Nowhere

Absence of Longterm Perspective

As surrogate owners, the failure of boards to establish a clear and distant vision for the district is likely the most serious of all leadership deficiencies. This short-term perspective often places the board's visionary horizon within the reading range of the unaided eye.

In extremes, *visioning* for some boards, is contained within the short span between now and the next election or appointment of committee members. Some consider next quarter or next month a serious priority for discussion; and the minutes of almost every board will recount its frequently protracted hashing out of last month's financial statement. These boards can toss a stone over their horizons and hit nothing of value on the other side.

Raymond said his board's *strategic plan* for tomorrow looked exactly like today. There's nothing wrong with that if you are trapped in a time loop as he suggests; however, every board trustee will agree that in today's ever-changing world, the future does not abide in the status quo.

Dr. Bogard says, "We must create the future, or we will become its victims." (personal correspondence)

Boards put up a good superficial argument, contending that *planning years into the future* sounds good; but how good can that plan possibly be. With a capricious legislature holding the purse strings, the board is discreetly loathe to commit itself to long-term projects that might have to be scrapped in mid-stream.

They further argue that it is unfair for a sitting board to bind future trustees to expenditures they might find difficult to fulfill, or otherwise be unwilling to accommodate years ahead.

Because of unstable tax-base prerogatives, many activities are subject to unplanned alteration within the budget year. Using today's governance standard, these trustees' position on this does seem to have merit.

However, under the paradigm of Policy Governance, school boards find themselves observing the future much farther downrange than this. So distant, in fact, that it is not *planning* in the same sense of the word. "Developing the vision" is a more accurate depiction of the board's contribution to planning – and the concept it provides becomes a lighthouse toward which the administration can steer. In Carver's words, "Boards produce the vision toward which plans plan."

The board's plan – that ideal and even utopian contrivance of the district's future – will not be affected by legislative flip-flops with the same calibration as are those administrative programs needed to bring it to pass. Having to modify programs, about which the board is currently concerned, is a hindrance that competent staffs are accustomed to dealing with.

Abdication of Mission

Board Gives Away Farm to Farmhand

Raymond said, "If I moved in the direction I thought

they wanted me to go, they would come back and say it was the wrong direction. If I moved left, they wanted me to the right. If I moved right, they wanted me to the left."

Raymond was voicing the wrong complaint. His protest should *not* have been that the board didn't approve of the direction he chose. But rather, the board had never given him the target to shoot at in the first place. He didn't even know where the target was.

If Raymond's board had given him a word picture of its vision for what the school district should be, then there could have been only one direction for him to go: Toward that vision. With half a brain, even he couldn't have missed.

You can't drive from Houston to Dallas unless you go North.

Consider a sharecropper who leaves the choice to the field hand for which crops to plant next year. If the farmer is working the land as trustee for someone else – as the school board's role is in relation to its owners – then he demonstrates irresponsible concern for the owner's assets.

Yet boards commonly abdicate their primary opportunity for leadership by failing to define the organization's destination or expected beneficial results, leaving it up to the executive to "lead" in the direction he or she hopes will take them there.

Dr. Bogard says, "It's as if you were to jump into the back seat of a taxi and tell the driver to take me somewhere. The driver asks where in particular; and you tell him that it doesn't matter at this point. 'Just start driving in some direction and I'll tell you if it's not the right one'."

The paradox then develops, that no one seems eager to claim the job. Staff is truly not empowered to do so, and the board seems unable or unwilling to take the challenge.

Boards will contest this charge by citing the clarity of their hiring interview when the superintendent accepted the job.

"The one important thing we hired him for," they will say, "was to lead the district. That's what he's paid to do, and that's what we expect of him."

The prerogative for making visionary decisions should lie with the elected body. The trustees were the ones chosen to represent the owners of the district. In the last school board election how many votes were cast for the superintendent?

This concept often finds disfavor with superintendents who are trying to work with an undisciplined board loudly divided between "right" and "left" factions of the ideological spectrum. The administrator sees the possibility of one or the other "extremist" faction gaining control of the board through the electoral process, suddenly leaving him/her bound to serve unfavorable ideological whims. That is, forced to lead the district toward a destination of which he or she disapproves.

As public opinion invariably vacillates, the certainty of this happening is imminent at some time or other – regardless of the nature of the governance system being used – for the board is the trustee owner of the district and is entitled to expect loyalty from its employees. No one suggests that a superintendent be compelled to administer policies contrary to his or her own personal beliefs. Yet, this hard choice is apt to present itself in the lives of all of us.

The position of Superintendent should not be a political one, but one of management and the administration of the district's mission. As such, the position's responsibility is to serve the board's leadership commands. If, for ideological reasons, the executive finds he or she can no longer do that, then – as in the corporate world – that hard choice has to be made.

Mature professionals are conditioned to cope with those situations, for they are common to one's ascent up the ladder of success. However, unique problems arise for administrators when:

1. No clear statement of those leadership commands are uttered by the board, and the superintendent must then try and please both sides of the aisle; or:
2. A clear policy is stated by the board majority, but the superintendent must continue to contend with buffeting interference from that vocal minority opinion.

Policy Governance does not forbid or discourage diverse opinion on the board; in fact, the model stresses its importance as indicative of complete district representation. However, the board has an obligation as a body to protect its Chief Administrator – from the board as individuals. Therefore, (as mentioned previously) the board should speak with one voice, not seven, or even three or two – and to do so with policies which reflect the majority opinion determined by a duly generated vote of those members participating. That "one voice" is the only statement of destination that the administrator should hear and then lead the district toward.

This does not mean that the other voices must then cease; but they are voices to which the superintendent owes nothing more than common professional courtesy. If the dissenting group wishes to continue pursuit of its agenda, its recourse is to the owners' ears and to those of their colleagues on the board. Not to those of the superintendent.

He or she now has marching orders and should follow them until instructed otherwise by the board as a body.

The Switching of Roles

Administrative staffs will sometimes take the initiative and bring to the board a so-called *Plan of Direction*. As often as not this project might be at the board's behest – where it has asked its staff to obtain input from the ownership, and to bring a recommendation to the board. This is the sort of working relationship that was experienced by the Atlantic Coast State superintendent whose taped interview I mentioned earlier.

In this example, the document is accompanied by a statement from the administrator, saying something like, "From our constituent input, we recommend that this is the direction the organization should be headed."

The staff member will then place the plan on the table. The board might then carefully peruse the plan, approve it, of course – or make a few changes and then approve it – and take credit for this great stroke of leadership.

If history is indeed a repeater, the board will then elbow the superintendent aside and diligently set about to devise the programs and procedures by which the plan can be administered so the district can move in the direction the wise superintendent has chosen.

Now we have a complete turnabout of roles. Staff has partially usurped the board leadership role by deciding the organization's *direction*, and the board has wasted the talents of a perfectly capable administrator by decreeing the programs needed to get going in *that direction*.

Usually, when a board does settle down to deliberate the future, it will produce a plan burgeoned by the prescription of administrative activity it deems necessary to take the district in a direction to nowhere specific.

Lacking a suitable governance vehicle to move discussion beyond the short visual horizon and the allure of trivia, it will then involve itself in the busyness of staff programs. Emphasis will always be on the programs and projects themselves, with little attention given to the examination of what human need is to be met by someone because of the school's existence.

Main significance will be attached to the busyness of staff. And the expected results – if stated at all – will be judged not by which human needs are met and for whom; but by how well they managed their programs.

In this setting, the superintendent must accept having the administrative plan handed to him by a dedicated part-time group which has followed the only route it knows in attempting to affirm its role as leader.

Now the superintendent has the direction. But he still doesn't know the destination.

Imagine what would happen if I came home and informed my wife that I had decided we should move?

She would wince and ask me, "Where?"

I would say, "North."

She would ask, "Where north? Do you mean Dallas? Chicago? Canada? How far north? How will we know when we get there if we haven't decided where *there* is and what *there* is supposed to look like?"

A destination and a direction are not the same thing.

Absense of Effective Monitoring

Of the important things a board must do to maintain accountability, monitoring is that which it does most poorly.

During the conversation with Raymond, he said the board got regular reports on everything the staff did. It was one of the ways he would discover that he was going in the wrong direction.

It is common for boards to burden themselves by poring over staff reports; and if, as in Raymond's case, the board was alerted to an errant administrative move, then it would be hard to convince it that the time and effort had not been well spent.

A board will contend that if it is legally accountable for everything that goes on in the organization, shouldn't it then be driven to monitor the goings-on with the eye of the watchdog that the public views it as being?

It is true that the ownership often views the board as a watchdog; and boards can see themselves as watchdogs if they choose. But, being a watchdog is not a very high calling. The eminent bearing of a school board trustee is loftier than that of a trained Doberman or hall monitor in a men's college dormitory.

Certainly, the taxpayers expect elected officials to be good stewards; and to honor that expectation, the board must ensure both fiscal and directional integrity. Under the conventional system of governance, the requirement of detailed staff reports in order to stay informed of what is going on, has been a prime method of confirming that integrity.

There is a better way.

The Beat Goes On

These board shortcomings are themselves perpetuated by a flawed process of Orientation. When new members are elected to the board, a queue of staff usually arrives to describe the projects and activities that are currently operating in the district. This may be followed by a projection of what administration hopes to accomplish in the next few semesters.

The natural result is that the new board member leaves the table with a terrific feeling of relief. Whew! Now, he or she feels they know what the job is all about. It's about projects and programs and the *busyness* of staff. And about what the administration has looming – just over the *short term horizon.*

The exigency of weak fiscal control and the board's reactive approach to problem solving contribute to support John Carver's assertion that, "The governance of public education is inadequate...and is not up to the task."

In his personal paper, A NEW STANDARD OF GOVERNANCE FOR PUBLIC EDUCATION, Carver writes: "There are many problems faced by school boards. But the *meta*problem unaddressed year after year is the difficulty of tapping the strategic leadership of the board. Endless *tinkering* with the internal workings of our schools (curriculum, techniques, grading, etc.) consumes everyone's interest and passion, while an incompetent leadership mechanism goes virtually unexamined."

Under the present system, boards are neither able to fully exploit the collective nor individual wisdom gathered around today's board table. Carver contends that the energy and depth of this wisdom is simply too valuable to waste. Policy Governance presents a new and powerful way of tapping into that quality of wisdom, which is born of human experience and erudition. – And to do so in a way that empowers both board and staff.

CHAPTER FIVE

THE CALL GOES OUT
FOR CHANGE

Boards, far from being unaware of the flaws that permeate their processes, sometimes shake their collective heads in the same consternation as does the governance missionary. Often this is done in private, but often as not it isn't. Concerned chairpersons may pound the table and call for an end to a trivial discussion and demand adherence to matters of greater import. Dedicated trustees bring motions to the floor in an effort to *"realign the board's purpose and heading"*

Board members often come away from the table in despair. How could we have spent so much time in this meeting, they ask themselves, and gotten so little accomplished? Yes, we need to realign the board's purpose and heading; but exactly what should that heading be? Surely, we all want the same degree of excellence for our children. Why can't we agree where we're going and then arrive on the same page? We need to consider the school district's mission and somehow clearly define that vision for our staff to work toward. But how do we do that? Is it because some of us don't share the same vision?

Former school board president Dr. Gregory Bogard had this to say: "Most of the board members I have known had a vision, all right; but that vision was only of the past. But, why shouldn't they? After all, most were well educated men and women; and the past is what is taught in school. Those who went to college were even deeper in the rut.

"I, myself, originally sought membership on the board and was encouraged to help keep the status quo. After a while I began thinking about the future and realized that without a blueprint of the future we cannot create it.

"Others on the board wanted to run the district hands-on, like they ran their businesses. They were the most interesting ones to watch – until they, themselves, filed for bankruptcy."

Asked if he would ever serve again as board president, Bogard said, "Not unless I had something new to bring to the board – and not unless I had an audience who could hear."

Many board members have new things to say; but is anyone listening?

Yes; and as a result of this awareness, board training has received renewed attention. State legislatures set standards requiring specified board training hours. But board training is often not only unproductive, but in fact (and here's that word again), counterproductive. For in their zeal to get better at what they do, boards are taught – even inspired – to do the wrong things better. Few, if any, fail to accomplish that goal.

Because the concept of this training is relatively new on the scene, glaring vacancies and omissions exist. Arzell Ball has worked with scores of boards during his long career, and points to some areas he feels should be addressed by board members' training: (personal correspondence)

He suggests a basic knowledge of State-school finance including yearly updates of changes, as well as knowledge of the education changes made by the legislature. A seminar on these subjects after each legislative session would be his suggestion.

He also recommends updates on student demographics because "with change in that index comes diversity and a need for adaptations of teaching methods."

So much does Carver agree with the board's need to remain informed, that his model specifically calls for policy which requires administration to inform the board's wisdom as part of its ongoing presentation of "decision making information"

At first, veteran superintendents might find Carver's response to this problem a bit unsettling because it seems to suggest an increase in pressure on the information pipeline that is already flowing to the board from the administrative data mill. However, if the category of data is elevated and restricted to the type needed for the board to make proactive governance decisions, then that superfluous flow will be greatly decreased.

Decision making information will be discussed in a later chapter, as it is information that is necessary for the board to do its own job. In the brief example stated above, the "adaptation of teaching methods", is a means issue that will be under the purview of administration, with the board's concern being addressed at a higher – or governance – level. Changes in demographics, however, are important to the board as it goes to the matter of, whom are we representing, and what changes in values are representative of that diversity?

Most information being generated and given to the board nowadays does not fall into this category at all, but rather the opposite; as most of it is information that *administration uses to make its decisions and do its job.* I ask you, of what benefit is it to the board to receive and cram on this category of information?

Board and staff are two separate entities with two different job outputs. And although we know this and espouse it in our daily speech, when we sit down at the table, we act as if we, the board, are simply staff one step higher. This *"Super Staff"* rut that boards find themselves in is what keeps the data mill churning. District leadership does not lie at the level of staff, but at that of the board of governors.

Dr. Ball includes in his list, a suggestion that board training should include, "Defining the job description of the Board member and helping him/her, and the public understand the roles of the board and of the superintendent."

He is certainly correct. If the average trustee were to write his or her own personal description of the board job, it might read like the combined jobs of everyone from superintendent to the manager of the bus barn – with the finance officer and human services manager sandwiched in between.

Dr. Michal Larraine Rosenberger, Ph.D., an independent consultant, demonstrates the extent to which a trustee must go – under the present system – in order to provide good board participation. In an article published in the NSBA Newsletter (reprinted with permission of author), she asks the question: "What role requires the knowledge of five PH.D.'s, the personal qualities of a diplomat, team skills of a NFL champion, is subject to local pressures, state and federal mandates, up to 40 hours a week of personal time, and the ability to perform flawlessly in public?"

Her answer, "Membership on the local school board."

She expresses the turbulent educational environment that the new board member is suddenly thrust into when elected. Things such as changing demographics and economic factors, increasing state and federal controls and, "A plethora of school improvement programs and strategies".

She continues by listing such things as, superintendent evaluation, goal and policy development, adoption and review, financial concerns, outside mandates from the state and federal level, facilities management, educational programs and things such as site-based decision making.

Whew!

Surely, our forebearers – the sagacious souls who originated the idea of having a school board in the first place – did not envision our taking on all these combined chores and cramming them into a two-hour meeting once or twice a month. Their naive board design may have worked well in the days of the one-room school house, or for the district with superintendent/principal rolled into one and with two or three teachers to handle a few dozen kids.

Perhaps if they were to conceive their brainchild in today's volatile educational setting, they would bring something quite different into the world. For we are headed toward the year 2000. Can we enter the 21st Century with 19th-Century governance techniques?

Continues Rosenberger, "As the operation of educational institutions continually becomes more complex, the skillful leadership and teamwork of the board of trustees and the superintendent are essential. They must be able to collaborate effectively in identifying the problems and needs of the community, achieve a working consensus on goals and priorities, agree on ways and means to implement the agreed-upon goals, and collaborate effectively on the required actions."

She fortifies Dr. Ball's suggestion that the public somehow be educated as to the roles of both board and superintendent, as she writes, "Unfortunately, instead of informing citizens of this ambiguous, complex and ever-changing role, the job description is simple, almost naive."

Her short, five point list of the board members' role is a vast improvement over current thinking, and serves to concentrate the board's attention away from administration and toward governance.

1. Hire and evaluate the superintendent and delegate all administrative duties
2. Approve the district's budget and set the tax rate
3. Adopt goals and evaluate outcomes
4. Adopt and evaluate policies
5. Communicate with the community

By directing the board's efforts toward broad policy adoption and calling for delegation of all administrative duties to those for whom those duties were intended, the board's chances of going awry are narrowed. In Chapter Eight, Carver's model will take it a step further and lower the odds even more.

Her point number (5) also lines up with Dr. Ball's contention. It is no accident that both these educators, observing the problem from disparate positions, see the same needs – that somehow the board must find a way to link up with its ownership and open channels of communication.

As to hindrances to board leadership, Rosenberger further observes that, "Personal challenges to effective performance come even before election if the candidate is unaware that a trustee has no individual power or is oblivious to legal, judicial, and financial constraints. The school board may be embarrassed or compromised by a novice attempting to save face with her constituency."

Dr. Gregory Bogard (personal correspondence) points to the problem from his own observation: "Many trustees do absolutely nothing to educate themselves for years on end while they hold their seats. Many are single issue politicians with single issue agendas. Even if they get their agendas passed, they still have years to serve and are there to deter the opportunity for vision and creativity that might have been available to the rest of the board."

Superintendent Ball is a man who has long trod the trenches of school administration and has a suggestion that might obviate these conditions. He makes the point that perhaps the district should offer annual training for board candidates as well as present board members, and further suggests that new members be assigned a partner who is an experienced board trustee.

Rosenberger concurs that board members are able to learn their roles more easily when they have access to an experienced trustee to serve as mentor. (Rosenberger, published paper: What Does an Effective Board Member Need to Know?)

Of today's board setting, she writes, "We cannot expect trustees to be instantly competent and knowledgeable... Every board member must quickly become a financial whiz, building contractor, personnel specialist, and media and public relations expert...."

In today's setting, she is right on the mark. However, Policy Governance asks the question: Why must this be so?

Why is a board trustee expected to be as conversant in matters of finance, construction, etc., as the competent people whom the district is paying to know and do those things? Must the owner of a trucking company be a certified diesel mechanic? Must the President of the United States be professionally schooled in military tactics and strategy in order to assume the role of Commander In Chief? Is an airline pilot required to know the intricate engineering details of his aircraft's electronic schematic? Could he be expected to tell the air controllers how to vector the traffic? Must he understand how the baggage is handled at the new Denver Airport?

These suggestions may sound burlesque at first glance, or even laughable; but for board trustees to be seriously expected to become expert in the myriad matters handled daily – moment by moment – by administration is equally amusing. I would suggest that few superintendents are that capable. Certainly, board members should be well informed people, but they should be well informed about the right things.

Many trustees and professional board watchers have observed the same as Bogard, Ball and Rosenberger; and have also weighed in with advice and counsel for boards which are in need of help. But this advice fits the general stock of reaction that has plagued boards in other areas of governance. That is, it prescribes a specific remedy to counteract whatever problem the board experiences at the time.

This *problem-based prescription* (BTMAD p.15), as Carver calls it, seldom works because it sows the seed for the next crop of trouble to sprout. Dr. Deming's eye-opening experiments in the principles of error compensation clearly demonstrated the fallacy of problem-based prescription as an elixir for curing ailments in management and process control. Continual use of these types of reactive remedies invariably leads the project awry.

In her diagnosis of System Flaws, published in the AASA publication, *The School Administrator* (reprinted with permission of author), Dr. Rosenberger agrees with Bogard's observation. In addressing reasons for lack of board leadership, she writes: "Personal agendas, idiosyncrasies, and self-serving behaviors are relatively easy to identify and are usually targeted as the primary problem. However total quality management (TQM) experts inform us that errors in performance most often result from flawed systems, not individuals. If that is true, then identifying, managing or removing the flaws or impediments should improve the quality of governance."

In a previous chapter I compared the board's well-meaning involvement in administration to the action of a toddler dashing into a flock of sparrows. The utilization of remedies based on the problem at hand might be compared to the child's mother instructing the tot to go chase the birds from the flower beds. The child chases the terrified birds who fly up and alight in the tree above, and the problem is temporarily solved. However, the mother has now created a new and greater difficulty – that of cleaning bird droppings from the child.

Problem-based prescriptions for board leadership are methods that do not work in the arena of management. What would cause one to believe they could nurse an ailing board back to health? Rather than this piecemeal approach to wellness, the remedy needed – as Dr. Rosenberger's article seems to indicate – is a change in the system. And, although she makes no endorsement of the Policy Governance model in her article, such change should be to a paradigm especially designed for the circumstances and requirements, not of management, but of governance.

Paradigm

Paradigm is a funny looking word. Someone with the educational background of the State secondary school system I attended might have trouble pronouncing it.

Paradigm means a particular way of looking at something; or a subjective viewpoint. Each of us has thousands of paradigms about just as many sundry things varying from mild opinions on sports to stiff theological convictions. The way we traditionally view the job of the school board is one of those paradigms. We have a way of looking at it that has been unchanged in our lifetime; and unless there is a shift in paradigm, those who will someday refer to us as their ancestors will bring to the board table the same archaic governance slant.

Carver says it is time for that paradigm shift.

Paradigm Shift

Acquiring knowledge by means of a shift in paradigm is different from the way people are accustomed to learning — as most learning takes place incrementally, where we learn a process and then spend additional study time adding to that knowledge. A linguist, for instance, could add more and more languages to his repertoire; and that would be incremental learning. But, if a fever were to leave him mute, without sight and hearing, he might be forced to learn to communicate telepathically. That would require a paradigm shift.

A Nineteenth-Century watchmaker could add to his craft incrementally by learning more about how to make tinier and tinier wheels, cogs and jewels. If he were suddenly vaulted into the 1990's and came face to face with the quartz crystal, it would require a shift in paradigm for him to grasp it.

People can become trapped by the particular paradigm they inhabit; and the story is told of a hapless group of Swiss who saw the quartz crystal on display at an exposition and sluffed it off as a passing fad. Now, world leadership in watchmaking has moved farther east from Switzerland, hasn't it?

The Paradigm Trap

A number of years ago I met a young student from an inner-city school district, who introduced himself to me as *Dr. Worm.* He wore the latest fad haircut, a colorful tee-shirt extolling his favorite rock group, and a large, odd-shaped wooden amulet dangling from around his neck.

We chatted for a while, and then I asked the *Worm Doctor* where he got his unusual name.

He lifted the wooden amulet from his chest and extended it out for me to see. It was a gift from his girl-friend, he said; and I craned my neck to look.

"It's an inchworm," said Dr. Worm. "She gave it to me before she went away to college, and I think it really says what kind of person I am."

"How so?" I asked.

"Well, I inch along one day at a time and never get riled up about anything. That way I stay real cool."

I agreed it was a stellar attitude to take, and I took the amulet in my hand for a closer examination. There was a small rhinestone on one end that certainly looked as if it could be a worm's eye. But it wasn't.

In fact, the amulet wasn't even an inchworm. It was Omega.

Dr. Worm was trapped by his paradigm.

Gregory Bogard reminded me that when rail transportation became irrelevant to the American scene, huge and expensive terminal buildings continued to be built for another ten years. Many of them still exist as a testimony to our unwillingness to face the need for a change in paradigm.

He repeats a theory suggested by his good friend Mr. Rick Mercer, as to why people are so indisposed to change. Ten years ago we referred to the *animal instinct* as the driving force that caused migrating birds and herds of wild beasts to travel the same seasonal routes – even when large cities are built in their paths. The same term was used to explain the salmon's upstream death swim to the place of its birth.

In the 1990's we have renamed that process and now call it *genetic encoding.* It's in their DNA, we say.

Are Americans genetically coded to do the same things, or can we look and see what is not working and do something else? Says Bogard, "Our record is not good on the subject."

CHAPTER SIX

THE NEW PARADIGM OF POLICY GOVERNANCE

The Policy Governance Model is certainly a shift in paradigm, as no amount of incremental learning will place it in perspective. One cannot put new wine in old bottles by attaching Policy Governance concepts to the framework of a board's current governance system. For one to grasp the new ideal (which Carver asserts is not particularly novel at all), one must temporarily set aside or unlearn everything they know about board governance as it is called today, and try on a new pair of glasses.

An organization is known and recognized by the values that it espouses. The organization is what it believes in; and a school board which professes a certain character must demonstrate it through its values in the way it conducts itself, how it connects with those around it, and what it moves toward. For whatever those values are, they ultimately form the foundation supporting everything about the district. Of course, school boards know this. This is not a notion endemic only to boards, but is applicable in all walks of life. It's the kind of staid fiber from which the garment of enduring mettle is woven.

Here in Texas, the TEC statute states that: The board members shall contribute to the development of a statement of educational philosophy expressing the present and future needs of the community and the children therein which will reflect the philosophy of the board. So, as John

Carver asserts, many concepts of Policy Governance are indeed nothing new.

These "present and future needs", which Carver defines as ENDS – and what I alluded to as *the destination* that Raymond Doe's board had failed to specify – exemplify the product ideals of public education. Yet, we, as boards, in selecting the way in which we sit in trusteeship, typically glaze over those essential governance values, and go directly into the processes of prescribing the management MEANS. Then, as did our predecessors, we quickly unearth that sweetsop of *administrivia* and mire ourselves in it.

Carver writes (BTMAD p.194), "To make ENDS policies for a public school system, the board must become more sophisticated about the skills needed for personal and social success in the world to come."

When we consider Dr. Bogard's charge that during his tenure he witnessed many trustees doing nothing to educate themselves, we can immediately concur with Dr. Ball's opinion that more and better training for board members is vital.

The Power Game

Dr. Ball alludes to *the diminishing balance of power between the board and the superintendent* due to such things as "the short tenure of the typical superintendent, and the shifting of Federal and State educational mandates to the local level."

Superintendent Ball's years of experience and administrative wisdom made him keenly aware of the balance of power that exists between the board and administration. A superintendent who learns and understands this reality is able to enjoy a successful career and endure to reflect upon it from retirement. Under the current system, there is only so much power to go around, and a tug-of-war often develops between administration and the board, with the Federal Government acting – perhaps unawares – as power broker in that *balance of power.*

This happens because the current system assumes a zero sum balance. When control shifts from the Federal level to those of local boards – allowing those boards choices where previously they had none – some programs, dear to administration, will no longer be protected by those mandates. The gain of power by one entity will have resulted, and be perceived, as a loss for another.

Such a system is, of course, counterproductive, as it casts board and staff in roles of contention – and the district as a house divided against itself.

Dr. Ball's earlier statement, calling for a better definition of the Board's job and that of the superintendent is extremely pertinent. He is correct, as most board members truly do not know what the job of the board is, and what their governing responsibilities are as trustees. Hence, this tug-of-war as board and administration often end up trying to do the same job, with the painting of the big picture left untouched.

The Big Picture

Boards which allow themselves candor may admit that one reason they falter at this bold step and fail to fully express and pursue their values in terms of what specific benefits are to be attained by the children because of the school's involvement, is that they simply don't know how. This is understandable, because ferreting out these ideals so as to develop a word picture of the board's vision for the district is not an easy thing to do.

Sure, as governance consultants, we can stress its importance, because we don't have to do it. In fact, we can't do it. I can no more paint a picture of another person's vision for their school district than I can walk across my filled swimming pool – particularly since the pool is eight feet deep, and the picture I would be asked to paint is based on the values and perspectives of that other person.

However, with careful thought and deliberation, trustees can paint this picture, and it's done by the same principles that are pervasive throughout the Policy Governance Model. Starting at the broadest level of vision – the Mega-Vision – and with the broad brush strokes of foresight and wisdom, the big picture will encompass those values which tell of our reason for the school's existence. What is in our minds for having and maintaining the school? Who is to benefit from it, and what are those benefits to be?

It may take some doing; but when completed, the mission – far from being something tacked on the wall like a decorative macrame to which the board can point with pride to visiting dignitaries – will represent almost everything about which the board will and should obsess for its duration.

The MEANS Oriented Mission

A more plausible reason for the board's failure to do this is the "path of least resistance" syndrome, where a board chooses to spend its visionary energy specifying the *means* because they are easier to measure. The index of pupil-day ratio expenditure, is a clear example of a *means* that districts methodically use to measure their progress.

Pupil-day measurement is a fine tool for management; but tells us nothing about the quality of benefits obtained by the child himself.

In determining the strategic path a district will be going over the long term, it is notably more important that the board choose the proper ENDS values to voice, than that it be able to measure those values with exactness. To violate this principle is akin to the old canard about the man who lost his half-dollar piece in the middle of the block, but chose to look for it at the corner under the street lamp because the light was better there.

The Mission Pledge of Allegiance

Other boards may feel they have in fact already expressed their values through their having saluted the mission statement that was placed on the wall by some board in the past.

The highest calling of *today's* school board is to define and redefine the reason for the school's existence and to juxtapose that purpose with its visionary blueprint for the district's future. As I said earlier, why did we decide to build a school in the first place? Which human needs did we wish to have met, or which inhumane circumstances alleviated, and for whom? Are those still our values today? Are they really worth paying money for, and if so, how much?

These questions present a challenge to many boards because it draws them up from the tempting preoccupation with staff activity and causes the juices of leadership at the governance level to begin flowing. But a different quandary now arises, as boards discover that stating these things is not easy to do.

Dr. Don W. Hooper, Superintendent of Fort Bend Independent School District wrote, "But, while we continue to strive for academic excellence, we cannot forget an equally important part of the child that needs our focus. For too many years, we have been afraid in public education to focus on the developmental side of the child; the side of that child that will enable him to take his knowledge and become a productive citizen in our society. Without that balance of character development and academic achievement, we have not fulfilled our responsibility to the children, or to our society.

"...Our goal should be that each child leaves our schools a life-long learner and a good citizen. It's an ambitious goal to accomplish." (Reprinted with permission from INSIDE FORT BEND SCHOOLS, Feb. 1995).

Notice in this statement, Dr. Hooper stresses what benefits the students will receive: That level of thought should be foremost. The board's eye should always be on that high mark, forever obsessing with what good will be obtained by the student, rather than the methods the superintendent might put into action in order that the child might obtain it.

Some will say, "What's so *avant-garde* about that? Many school districts have mission statements which embody those very phrases. Obviously, their boards are doing their jobs well."

I differ with that. For while it is true, most mission statements do embody the essence of what should be done for the child, those intentions are almost always cloaked in just that: what the district will be intent on doing, instead of what the child will be receiving.

It may sound flippant, but I use as example, the difference between teaching and learning. The teacher can teach all day long; but if the child does not learn, then neither of them have earned promotion. In this single restricted example, a purpose statement would best be centered on the child's learning rather than on the district's teaching.

Certainly you cannot have learning unless you first have teaching; but the mission's emphasis should be on the former.

Dr. Hooper says that, "I firmly believe that every child can learn." Whether that assessment be true or not will be debated. However, it is absolutely imperative that school districts, their boards and their administrators *"firmly believe"* it is.

Therefore, the expandable theory goes further – into the things Dr. Hooper expressed in his article. It should first be what we wish the child to receive from our efforts that should occupy the board's thinking. Those issues are the board's province to decide. How to ensure that the child receives and claims those benefits is the job of a competent administrator.

If such a statement is a declaration of the district's mission and is so called, that is good. But, the importance does not lie in what it is called, but rather in what it has to say.

Another concern is that, assuming such a statement of purpose is actually an expression by the board and not simply a document drafted by staff for the board to endorse in assent, these lofty ideals are seldom revisited. Superintendent Hooper does well in restating them – and then taking it a bold step beyond: "With the cooperative efforts of staff, parents and our students, it's a goal that can be reached."

How to do it

To express the values of an organization – and therefore develop governing policies about those values – Carver's method departs obliquely from the language of management and utilizes the language of governance.

Consider a school district's administrative challenges: asset protection and management, liquidity requirements, personnel procedures, purchasing and inventory, for instance. These are things over which the board must somehow ensure its accountability without impeding the Teflon mechanisms of good management.

Consider also the board's view of the school district's outlook and potential – those values we have briefly visited above. Consider the vast activities agenda that the staff envisions will be necessary to bring that vision to fruition, as the range extends from the profound to the mundane.

The school board as individual members certainly has certain priorities, misgivings and personal *pets* among all of these goings-on (remember Dr. Bogard's words as to the personal agendas some board members bring to the table). And problems arise when those individual members – or the board as a whole – attempt to apply their personal values to choosing those staff means and the methods by which they will be carried out. For some board members, the multiplicity of items and ways to bring this about may look like a shopping list for "Indiana Jones".

A way must be found to determine what the board as a *whole body* values as the thing or things these programs and activities will produce for the students – and, therefore, for the district. And as for the activities themselves, to find a way of obtaining that assurance of ethical and responsible compliance by staff, which the board must be able to demonstrate to the ownership.

The language of management might refer to these indices in terms of goals, aims and objectives, etc. Carver's model, however – in order that all these board concerns can be safely placed beneath the umbrella of accountability – uses a specialized nomenclature to codify each into one of two distinct groups which he calls *ENDS and MEANS.*

You may ask, what's so specialized and distinct about the terms ENDS and MEANS? Everyone in management uses those words as much if not more than they do goals and objectives. We use them in our everyday lives to express our hopes, our expectations and our plans for self-achievement. Ends and means is as common a duo as grass and seed: the grass being the end result you desire, and the seed, the means of obtaining it.

The special utility – in Policy Governance – of ENDS and MEANS, lies not in the words themselves, but in the precise definitions Carver has assigned them and the contrasting ways the board will address each group.

The distinction of Ends and Means

An ENDS issue – as I alluded to earlier – is any issue the organization will deal with having to do with what human need will be met for which persons (outside the immediate organization, i.e., board and staff); and at what cost. In the case of schools, the issue asks, what are the benefits that will be received by the students? And how much is this worth?

If this definition seems overly elementary, then consider the simplicity of the following: MEANS are everything else.

CHAPTER SEVEN

ENDS AND MEANS

Input From Customers and Owners

When was the last time your board conducted a face-to-face dialogue with its customers as to what educational ENDS those parents wish the board to purchase for the district. When has it last held a full discussion of these matters with its owners? If that sounds redundant, let me explain that customers and owners – although they can be the same people – are not necessarily so.

Inclusively, as taxpayers in a school district, exist both owners and customers. I for example, am a taxpayer and, therefore am an owner of the school district in which I reside. However, I am not a customer of the district because I do not have children going through the grades. My son has four girls; he is a customer as well as an owner. In a public forum, the input from him, as a customer, would be radically different from that which the board would get from me.

As a customer, he might be complaining about such matters as the school bus coming too late or too early; about it stopping in the wrong place; about the poor quality of food served to the students; or about his child not being given a proper opportunity to compete for cheerleader. He might even threaten to sue if something isn't done. These are customer complaints, and boards hear them all the time. And when so, they immediately repair to their reactive stance and purpose to, *"do something about it"*.

As an owner, however, I would be giving ownership input. Perhaps complaining about my taxes being too high, and too much money spent on bells and whistles and not enough on teachers. I might even pound the podium and threaten to *"make my voice heard at the ballot box"*. Boards also hear these kinds of complaints often and, except during board elections, are the ones they pay least attention to.

Did you notice that none of this owner/customer input shed any light for the board to know what skills, understandings and attitudes the school should bring about for the children? The issue of ENDS – what good for which people at what cost – was never mentioned.

How could it? It is likely the board never knew to ask.

The Mission Statement

I do not deny that school boards put much agonizing thought into these ideals. As I have already stated, most Purpose Statements ring loudly with a proclamation of those values. However, in its proclamation, the benefits – the ENDS – along with the board's good intentions, are all too often quickly denigrated by stating them in the context of MEANS.

That is to say that the benefits are expressed not by what the child will be achieving, but by what the district will be doing to provide that service or make that achievement available.

Admittedly this is not a deep study of Policy Governance, and Dr. Carver devotes many pages in his book to a more thorough examination of this unfortuitous detour by the board. Suffice it here to say that as time passes and the MEANS gain greater definition and stature in the reporting pecking order, they take on the ENDS persona and begin to be treated as such.

Let me reiterate the last point of the previous chapter. ENDS equate to the beneficial results – and MEANS are everything else. A very cursory list of MEANS might include:

1. The projects, programs and activities associated with bringing about those Ends.
2. The equipment we use (computers, telephones, busses, kitchen appliances, etc.)
3. Our buildings, gymnasiums and playgrounds.
4. Our staff, the way we train our staff, and our hiring practices.
5. The curriculum, the teachers and the daily schedule.
6. The budget, and the time, personnel and methods used to produce it.
7. The services we provide, and the methods we use to measure them.

MEANS, therefore, are everything *we either USE, DO, or PROVIDE* in the fulfillment of the ENDS mission. Obviously this list could be amplified at each classification, expanding the number of possible issues into the hundreds or thousands. But it would not change the reality: that if it isn't an ENDS, it's a MEANS.

I did not say that the board will deal with ends and the staff with means, because the board and the staff will each deal with both ends and means. And neither did I say that ends were ends because they were important and means were not important. John Carver's definition clearly points out that means are important because they must lead to the ends. And that in doing so, it is important that they do not violate principles of prudence and ethics that the board will have specified.

More about this will be said later in this chapter.

The ENDS/MEANS Masquerade

"In the absence of clear dictates about intended effects on the world (*children* – my insertion), a number of means come to be treated as if they were ends themselves." (John Carver – BTMAD p.59). Staffs will then get busy and begin to issue reports not about the welfare that the well-intended board wished to confer on the child, but about which kinds of programs will be used and about the tracking methods for measuring their own efficiency in taking the projects forward.

It happens so smoothly and without notice that in one glib turn of a word or two, emphasis on results will have been shifted from those who receive to those who give – from the donee to the donor. This method of measurement will then be used to justify everything from revenues to expenditures, and the true ENDS will in time disappear from the table, and, hence from the board's dialogue.

As an example, let's fabricate a bold purpose statement for a school district and see how easily this mistaken identity for ENDS and MEANS can come about:

PURPOSE

The mission of Faircity Independent School District is to provide our students with the opportunity to become life-long learners and productive citizens in a changing global society.

A concerned parent might look at this mission statement and say, "Simple and to the point. Who could ask for anything more?"

Granted, this is a "fantasy" statement produced by me to make a point; but the problem with this kind of mission statement is that it is MEANS oriented. Although it mentions the benefits intended for the child – lifelong learning and productive citizenship – it is watered down by the statement that the district will be *providing the opportunity* for those things to happen.

What if many or most of the students do not avail themselves of the *opportunity?* What if? What if? Remember, we said above that a MEANS was anything (a service) that we would be doing or providing.

If we make the opportunity to become productive citizens and lifelong learners available, and no one takes advantage of the opportunity, do we still give ourselves good marks for *Providing The Opportunity?* Well, we might, because we have worked very hard, haven't we? But the next question is: But, is it worth paying money for?

In the ENDS/MEANS Masquerade, the answer to that might be "YES", because we will have been measuring our success not by how much benefit the students received, but by how hard we worked at providing them *The Opportunity.*

We have fallen into the *opportunity* trap that Policy Governance warns against.

Perhaps a better, more ENDS oriented statement might be:

The mission of Faircity ISD is that all students of the District obtain the skills, abilities and attitudes to be lifelong learners and to be productive citizens who successfully compete in a changing global society.

It may seem as though I am splitting hairs; however, in this statement the wording emphasis is on the student's benefits to be obtained, and not on the district's diligence in providing them the opportunity to do so.

Under the previous mission statement, both the board and the administration can shed considerable culpability if the students fail to reach those lofty goals. For after all, everyone worked their fingers to the bone to provide the opportunity. They have the project data to prove it.

But, with the ENDS oriented statement, no matter how hard the district works to see it accomplished, it cannot escape blame for its failure to come about.

Of course, these outcomes will be harder to measure. But aren't the expected results worth it?

"The management principle that applies here is radically different from the academic one," says Carver. That is to affect the direction a district takes for the duration of its strategic vision, a primitive measure of the right thing beats a precise measure of the wrong thing.

Carver relates having observed a public school board spend a very long, cluttered meeting moving from one staff means issue to another, most of which were not very large. In the middle of this flurry of discussion was an agenda item, "concerning the outcome of extensive tests of reading ability throughout the system". The board spent only enough time to notice the item and acknowledge it with a few good words before moving immediately back to the administrivia. (BTMAD p.63)

Obviously, the import and relevance of those trivial matters were easier to measure.

Our kids deserve more.

Addressing ENDS and MEANS

The Chinese Boxes

Policies about ENDS

You remember Chinese Boxes. That small set of color-ful boxes you once got for Christmas as a child. The set was graduated in size so that each fit into the next larger one. By placing all of them inside each other until only one large box was visible, the entire set could be carted off to the toy box and stored with ease. None were left lying around for Father to kick in the night, or for Mother to scold about in the morning. Juvenescent as it may seem, this is the analogy that best describes the simplicity with which policy issues can be handled by the board.

The value issues of ENDS and MEANS, about which the board will draft its policies, are of both great and less importance, and of large and small dimensions. A board policy which addresses the largest value issue will house within it all smaller, relevant issues – making the dispo-sition of these smaller issues dependent upon the resolu-tion of each larger issue above it. The decision to take a vacation is a larger issue than deciding to go to the sea-shore or to the mountains. The latter cannot have been made without having first resolved the former.

Recognizing that values display this same concentric-ity, a board can examine and control the largest issue – as in the nested set of boxes. At this initial point the board is in control of the entire set (of issues), as all subsequent smaller sized issues are contained by the hands-on con-trol of the larger issue.

The largest ENDS issue represented by the largest box would likely be the district mission – although it need not be called that. The board will draft and affirm that broad statement, being careful to draft it in ENDS terminology and not in the language of activities or services provided, and then move down to the next level – further defining its intent as to what it wishes the district's educational endeavors to yield beneficial to the students. The board can come in as deeply as it wishes, pinpointing each issue with clear, succinct policy statements of what its vision is for the district.

Depending upon the depth of involvement the board wishes to impose, it can reach into the nested set and remove and deal with each of the smaller issues in their order of size. By going in one level at a time and deciding the next smallest issue along the way, it can examine each and decide at what depth it wishes to relinquish the decision-making authority to its administrator.

There will come a point beyond which the board will find it too menial an area for its governing prerogatives. At this level it can surrender further defining of its ENDS policies into the hands of its administrator who will use his or her reasonable interpretation of what the board has said in fleshing out what must be done, and deciding how to do it.

The board has now given up hands-on control of the smaller issues – leaving its staff free to make the smaller, day-to-day choices in its stead. Yet, it is still assured of governance control through staff's compliance with its basic policies.

The process continues down through the district *chain of command*, as the administrator then apportions the work through staff and down to the principal and into the instructional corps.

An analogy of this – an example Carver frequently uses

in his presentation of Policy Governance – would find an issue in perhaps the next to smallest box which asks the question: What will little Johnny Brown learn next Tuesday morning at 10:30 a.m.?

This is an ENDS issue, because it deals with what good (learning), for which person (Johnny Brown), and it carries with it a cost in the amount of time the teacher can allot – perhaps taking away from another child – in order for Johnny to learn.

Since this is an issue that the teacher will decide, it is obvious that somewhere between the largest box and the small one containing this issue, the board has relinquished control. It has decided and stated the larger value and come into greater detail as far as it chose; and at some point it has given authority to the administrator to make further interpretive decisions about students' learning – based on, and in line with what it has said at the higher level. The administrator has at some point given that interpretative authority to the principal, and it was then given to the teacher.

Moving to the larger scale, let's take a look at the fantasy Mission Statement of Faircity ISD, and see how it might be fleshed out:

The mission of Faircity ISD is that all students of the District obtain the skills, abilities and attitudes to be life-long learners and to be productive citizens who successfully compete in a changing global society.

The school board could hardly give this Carte Blanc broad statement to its administration with any degree of self-assurance that its interpretation would lead the district in the proper ENDS route. So, the next level of definition might say which skills, as in reading, math, English, science, etc., and to what degree the board wishes those skills to be obtained.

An inner city board might specify a higher priority for its students to achieve proficiency in the area of "spoken English"; while a school board from a bi-lingual area of the State might want its students to acquire a high proficiency in English, but fully retain knowledge and use of the native tongue.

In a "mixed-bag" school district with diverse demographics, the board might differentiate its priorities by concentrating attention for certain skills on students of a particular area.

The board could specify what those levels of proficiency were to be, for which particular students if applicable, or leave those choices to the superintendent to make. If the board were to address the matter of SAT or ACT scores, it might establish district-wide standards to which those scores must be elevated within a specified number of years. If the board makes the choice and assigns hard numbers to these priorities in terms of cost, then the latitude for interpretation becomes narrower.

This is a short example of a possible ENDS issue dealing with what the board said in its purpose statement about the students obtaining skills; and the list can be expanded in each area of skill that the board wishes to address. Since there is possibly an arm's-length list of ENDS issues to be dealt with by a school board, a book could likely be written on that alone.

Questionable Ends

Some trustees will shake their heads and exclaim, "But, is this all we want to do for our children? Skills are essential, but what about school yard safety? What about transportation safety? What about teacher safety? What about mandated nutritional school lunches, for goodness' sake? Doesn't the importance of these issues, and their relevance to education, merit the attention of the board? Where do these things fit into the picture?"

They are important issues, and they do deserve the board's attention through policy. However, let's make sure the board handles these issues the right way.

The board asks itself: Is safety an ENDS issue? If so, to what degree do we as a board wish to impose policy? If it is not and ENDS issue, why is it not? And if not, doesn't its importance – as the trustee asked – still merit our attention?

Obviously, safety is a benefit to the child – either at school or to and from. As is proper nutrition, if so mandated by the strings which hold onto the funds that are allocated for this purpose. But so is comfort through proper heating and air conditioning, proper lighting, smooth blackboards, designer desks and sanitary restrooms. All of these MEANS produce a kind of result which can be described as a benefit. Yet that kind of benefit or result does not necessarily ascribe ENDS value to it.

Perhaps we might decide that safety is an ENDS because of the degree of its importance. That is, it is more important than comfort, therefore, it is an ENDS. Not so.

We must ask ourselves the question: If we established a new school district today, would the safety of our children be the reason for establishing the school? Did our forbearers get together and say, "Let's establish a school district here so our kids can be safe?"

The answer to that is NO. The school district was established so that kids can *"obtain the skills, abilities and atti-*

tudes to be lifelong learners and to be productive citizens who successfully compete in a changing global society".

In order to obtain that result, the school district is expected to utilize particular common sense paths and provide certain humane services (remember, a MEANS is anything we either USE, DO, or PROVIDE in the fulfillment of the ENDS mission). And safety – as well as many of the other "benefits" I mentioned, is one of the services it is expected to provide.

John Carver had this to say in personal correspondence: "A system can have results which themselves are not stated ends. For example, we create schools so that kids can develop certain life capabilities. We do not create them so that kids can have a safe environment. A police department, of course, might be created in part for that latter outcome. In running schools, however, we do not want to create or allow an unsafe environment. In this way, safe environment is an ends issue for law enforcement, but not for schools.

"For schools, safety is a means issue. It is an important one necessary both (a) to preserve the ability to develop those capabilities and (b) to avoid the unethical and imprudent action of exposing them (children) to jeopardy. Hence, I'd say there's no doubt that safety is not an ends issue for schools, but a means issue."

The ease with which boards turn important means issues into ends is pervasive, and putting this angle of the ENDS/MEANS concept in perspective may require some thought. But the clear conclusion cannot be missed: safety – regardless of its importance – is simply another variation on the ENDS/MEANS Masquerade.

Yet, this still does not answer the trustee's question above, does it? "Doesn't the importance of these issues, and their relevance to education, merit the attention of the board?

Where do these things fit into the picture?"

Safety is an important issue and is something the district will be providing as part of the educational big picture. Since it is a MEANS, our cardinal rule of Policy Governance is that the board does not prescribe the methods for providing this important segment; however, this does not mean that the board will fail to address the issue and have no control or say-so as to how this means issue is carried out. The board will have much to say about it; and the way this is done – must be done – will be discussed a bit farther down in this chapter.

If we return to my fantasy school board of a few pages back where trustee "Lucille" was deeply involved in the daily lunch diet, we can see how proper separation of ENDS and MEANS would have relieved her of that prescriptive meddling. Since proper nutrition falls into the same category of issues as does safety, i.e., it is an important MEANS, we can see that she is out-of-line in prescribing the means or methods by which proper nutrition is meted out by administration.

Yet, let me make it clear that Lucille is not without input; in fact, her input is vast and is paramount to governance. But, that input should be holistic, as part of the board's *one voice* principle. And that *one voice* will express itself in the drafting of proactive policies which deal with the limits placed on staff actions. Those Executive Limitations policies will be discussed a bit farther along in this chapter.

Meddling – what is it?

In describing "Lucille's" improper use of the board's position, I again used the term "meddling". Simply trying to stay abreast of district progress and activity is not, in itself, meddling. Meddling, in this context means when the board jumps into a much smaller level of concern or begins to prescribe the means as Lucille has done.

So, the guiding tenet of Policy Governance is that the board can go as deeply into the set of issues as it wishes, as long as it goes in one level at a time and settles that issue before moving onto the next. And in all the vital areas of ENDS that the district must deal with, it is the board's choice to decide at which level it wishes to relinquishment that authority. But once it is relinquished, that authority should remain with the administration – unless the board wished to modify its own policy.

First Things First

The first challenge, then, is for trustees to hammer out their value differences up front and bring to staff a set of policies that is inclusive of the board's consummate values. This may not be an easy task for some groups – those which are chaired and subtly dominated by an especially opinionated president, or those which routinely defer to the opinions of one or two highly-respected members.

I am no more *"Lettered"* to advise boards in the intricate techniques for escaping these pitfalls and achieving effective board deliberation than would be any other outsider. And boards are far less apt to resent reproof from amongst their own ranks than from the pompous stance of a finger wagging governance consultant. Those techniques are best instructed by professionals who are proficient in group problem solving and adult conflict resolution. However, one need not have gone to *Deliberation School* to recognize the importance of bringing diversity of thought and opinion to the board discussion – since that same diversity exists in the homes and minds of those for whom we agreed to sit in trusteeship.

Secondly, the board must be willing to stand behind whatever its policy says. That commitment contains within it agreement by all trustees that the stated position of the board is the official position of the board. Individual board members may still disagree, but that dissension must not work to undermine the board's one-voice proclamation.

"A great deal of time and effort is spent by boards that bring diversity to resolution. Undermining that resolution once reached wastes trustees' commitment and muddies delegation to the *superintendent* (my italicized insertion – Carver/Mayhew, A New Vision of Board Leadership, ACCT, 1994, p. 42).

"The method requires trustees to settle their differences one level at a time, just as if they were components in a nested set. This level-at-a-time approach takes discipline while policy is being developed, to be sure, but pays great dividends in time saved later."

With respect to the ENDS issues, this turning loose of authority at a given level will manifest itself as permission for the administrator to make further judgments about those issues based on a *reasonable interpretation* of what the board has already said in its larger policy statement.

The Interpretation Paradox

All will agree that any wording of any policy will always be open to some degree of interpretation; that it is impossible to so finely hone a statement that will escape the opportunity for interpretation at some point. The key in the Policy Governance usage of this principle is, *"a reasonable interpretation"*.

If I asked my secretary to, "make me some Xerox copies" of a letter I had received, it would be open to interpretation. For instance, how many copies? If she brought me a half-dozen copies, it would be a reasonable interpretation of my request. But knowing my business needs as she does, if she brought me a hundred copies it would not be a reasonable interpretation.

In Policy Governance, *a reasonable interpretation* means that which a competent administrator, making a prudent person's judgment about a standing board policy, would conclude.

If that decision turned out not to find favor with the board, the burden might then be on the administrator to show that he or she had used a reasonable interpretation of the board's policy in making that decision – which honest and intelligent people can easily do. The decision might not have been one the board, itself, would have chosen to make. But if the decision was a reasonable interpretation of its policy, then the administrator stands on firm footing.

Notice that this principle does not say the superintendent's decision must please the board – and certainly not individual board members – but rather that it was made in compliance with the board's policy based on a reasonable interpretation thereof.

Beyond that, if dissatisfaction still exists, the problem lies not with the superintendent's decision, but with the board's policy being too loose or unclear – and therefore, open to more interpretation than the board can live with. The board now needs to modify its policy and tighten the latitude for interpretation.

Of course, it can always countermand the superintendent's decision. However, that rescindment must carry the understanding that there was nothing wrong with the superintendent's decision; but that the board had not expressed its policy clearly enough.

If we examine this concept at the smaller ENDS level where the teacher made the decision about little Johnny's needs, we find that it works perfectly well. Her decision, based on her reasonable interpretation of whatever "policy" the superintendent and principal had made, would have no trouble passing muster in the scheme of things. And so on up the ladder to the board.

Policies about MEANS

The text concerning this category of policies has been long in coming; but as you may have suspected, the same principle of nesting large and small issues also applies to the means that an administration will employ to achieve the ends. There are large means and there are small means, with all sizes in between; and within the concepts of the Policy Governance model, they also fit together like the nested set of Chinese Boxes. The important guiding principle here, however, lies in the dissimilarity with which ENDS and MEANS are addressed by the board.

The Positive Negative

With regard to the ENDS, the board will speak POSITIVELY, and will write policies at the broadest level which prescribe what those issues are. In addressing the means by which the staff will accomplish the board's vision, the board will also begin at the broadest level; however, in doing so, it will speak to those issues NEGATIVELY. In other words, the board will prescribe the ENDS by stating what must be done, but will PROSCRIBE the staff MEANS by stating the things which *must not* be done. – The things which it would find unacceptable.

It's as if the board were to say:

These are our ENDS desires, Mr. Superintendent – our vision of what we want the district to be for the sake of the children. We want you to accomplish these ENDS for us. We're not going to try and tell you how to do the job; you may use any means within the bounds of your knowledge and skill, and we won't tell you what to do. We're only going to tell you (set executive limits) the conduct that, if done, would not be all right by our standards. Now, they're not very many things – the list is short; but they represent the bounds of ethics and prudence that would be a reason for your termination if you did them.

Of course, the board *will* say this; but it will say it through the issuance of its Executive Limitation policies, and those policies which direct the board's own means and spell out its proactive governing style.

Executive Limitations

The knee-jerk reaction to this concept is discomfiting for boards because they do not wish to appear as negative *nay-sayers*. It is, for some, unseeming that the board should issue a list of no-no's to its staff. Yet, the positive aspects generated by this limiting verbiage allow for greater freedom and creativity, in that such freedom is clearly bounded by restraints of ethics and prudence within which administration is – and feels – empowered to act without board approval at every turn. Rather than the traditional *"Simon-Says"* method of board governance, and the intrusion and meddling it germinates, this short list of executive limitations removes the board's temptation to dabble prescriptively in staff means – and its implementation – by telling the superintendent how the staff is *not to do its job.*

At first, this may seem like an impossibility. A board might ask, "How can we possibly think of all the things that we don't want the superintendent to do? The list could be endless."

Yes, it could be. But if we begin with the largest no-no and come in to the next smallest, we quickly limit the range of prohibitive action severely. For example:

A limitations policy preamble might begin with a broad statement (remember the Chinese Boxes Principle) that the superintendent may not violate accepted standards for prudence and ethics. Surely, a reasonable interpretation of this is not difficult to defend; yet, such a statement has now covered *a multitude of sins.* The list of possible no-nos has suddenly gotten much shorter.

Doubtless, few boards will leave its superintendent so wide a latitude for action as in this example. Yet, Carver contends if a board were to say that and nothing more – and could be assured of compliance – it will have greatly reduced its anxiety level.

Most boards will choose to further define that preamble in each of the separate areas of concern by adding (going into the next smaller box) – as an example with regard to asset protection: "The superintendent may not allow assets to be unprotected, inadequately maintained nor unnecessarily risked". (Excerpt from CGD Guided Policy Development packet – Asset Protection example)

Further defining the issues of prudence and ethics, the board might then draft short statements – being careful that they be stated proscriptively – to address theft and casualty coverage, restrictions on unbonded personnel, exposure to claims of liability, and limitations on large ticket item purchases, etc.

When finished, this Executive Limitation policy about asset protection would likely have no more than nine or ten points on one single sheet of paper and comprise all of what the board would have to say at the governance level about the subject.

If the board felt that the main preamble which forbade imprudence and unethical administrative conduct was not sufficient to assure school yard safety and proper nutrition for the children, separate policies about those two issues could be drafted with the board narrowing the latitude for interpretation of its values to whatever extent it felt comfortable.

Following that, the superintendent would be empowered to use his or her reasonable interpretation thereof, and could then draft as many and varied management policies as necessary or desired in order to express that interpretation and disseminate it further to the staff.

But the board – as governor – has said all it need say.

This proactive/proscriptive process is repeated in each area where the board might have legitimate worry or concern: from financial planning to transportation of the children.

With most boards, these Executive Limitation policies can be drafted on as few as ten or fewer pages, with usually no more than four or five points per page. The result places a set of clear and concise policies at the board's fingertips, enabling it to govern with more fiscal assurance and greater administrative accountability – and freeing it for its elected leadership role.

The staff is now able to soar within this bounded freedom; to use its knowledge, its resourcefulness, and even its genius to accomplish the ENDS which have been clearly delineated and placed before them by the board's policies.

The Stability/Alterability of Policies

The empowerment and accountability concepts of Policy Governance have existed for years; it is their professional application which Carver's model outlines that makes them unique in governance. My mother, although she did not know them as such, used similar techniques in taking care of me more than four decades ago.

I recall that we had moved from a small town in Louisiana into a new home in Dallas, Texas – almost in the shadow of downtown. My mother wanted to make sure that I did not get into mischief in this unfamiliar neighborhood; but she also did not wish to dampen my excitement of living in a big city. Without knowing it, she created some ENDS and MEANS limitation policies that worked well for both of us.

"You can play on the sidewalk and have as much fun as you like," she said. "But I want you to be safe. So, these are the things I don't want you to do."

She said I couldn't play in the street; I couldn't play in other peoples' yards, and I couldn't go around the corner where she couldn't see me. Those were the limitations which I clearly understood.

And then she added a new exponent to the equation: "And I will be checking on you from time to time to see that you are all right." She let me know she would be monitoring me – not to try and catch me breaking the rules, but just to see how I was doing.

I was happy with this arrangement because I knew where my perimeter was. The list of no-no's she had given me was short, but it was all inclusive. It was the street and the end of our block. I was free to skate up and down the sidewalk as fast as I wanted; slam into our garage door and make as much noise as I wanted; and even write on the sidewalk with all that white, chalk rock that lay around everywhere. And I didn't worry that she might catch me doing something wrong, because I didn't intend to do so. I was a good kid; and her ENDS and MEANS worked perfectly.

The second day we were there I spied a little girl named Mickey who lived across the street; and I asked Mother if I could go across and play. She said okay and then added another limitation: "But don't go inside Mickey's house."

The system worked well until I decided to climb Mickey's tree in her front yard and then lost my footing and tumbled out.

My yelps brought Mother onto the scene, whereupon she took me home and found nothing broken. Luckily the short fence I fell astraddle broke my fall.

And neither had I broken any of her *don't-do-it* rules.

However, my reasonable interpretation of her policy necessitated her tightening the wording by adding another limitation: "Don't climb Mickey's tree."

The point made by this inane vignette is that the board has a right to adjust its policies, either tighter or more lax, at any time deemed necessary. If it finds through experience that its Executive Limitations Policies yield more latitude for reasonable interpretation than it originally planned, it can pencil in the change.

The board might find that its policy on financial condition is too open to liberal interpretation, allowing the possible imprudent liquidity of long term reserves. It might modify its Executive Limitation on Financial Condition to allay that possibility.

In contrast, it might discover that its limitation policy on compensation and benefits unduly ties the hands of administration in meeting market salaries for computer knowledgeable personnel.

It could then modify its policy to allow the superintendent greater latitude in negotiating with those candidates.

In both these cases the board's values will not have changed at all, which contributes to the stability aspect of Policy Governance. However, the range of interpretation will have been altered, either wider or more narrow, to fit the board's comfort zone – demonstrating the alterability of board policies.

From a monitoring standpoint, if its superintendent happens to be a poor tree climber, it can obtain greater comfort in that area by more closely monitoring what goes on in the jungle. If, however, the administrator turns out to be Tarzan incarnate, then the board might feel it can relax a bit and let him swing.

Whatever the board has said in policy, if needs be, can be unsaid; but it has an obligation to uphold staff's inculpability for whatever MEANS decisions were made thereunder, at the time.

"This method requires trustees to stand behind the words they have chosen to use. The commitment to own its own words extends both to the board's relationship with the

superintendent (my italicized inclusions), and to the board's relationship with the public. Since governance is a verbal job, saying what you mean and meaning what you say must be a credo."
(Carver/Mayhew, ANVOBL, ACCT 1994, p.43)

No Better Way

As boards move to a higher plateau of deliberation about matters of district governance, the ENDS/MEANS-distinction principle, far outstrips any other method for enabling them to properly handle and control both these important categories of issues. Care must be taken to understand that as the board is the owner of the district in trusteeship, it is, therefore, owner of both the ENDS and the MEANS, and must deal with and be responsible for the existence of each.

The power of Policy Governance rests in the disparate way (Positive/Negative) each is ingressed by board involvement.

Carver does not eliminate the management terms, goals and objectives, from the board vocabulary, as they are useful terms for establishing and ordering workload priority – and will still exist. For example, there will continue to be goals and objectives about both ends and means, as these terms find their useful application in the ENDS/MEANS distinction.

At the end of the first chapter I asked the rhetorical question, "What could be higher than being the Final Authority?"

Had Raymond's board drafted its prescriptive ENDS policies and then stipulated the executive MEANS limitations, it could have — in Carver's words — moved beyond the weak, reactive stance of being the final authority, and, "elevated itself to the leadership demeanor of a board of *Initial* Authority."

CHAPTER EIGHT

THE BOARD STATES ITS OWN MEANS

In the previous chapters we have discussed the board's need to ensure and demonstrate accountability for itself and its administration. We have discussed the differentiation of ENDS and MEANS, and the disparate ways in which each will be addressed by the board – by speaking positively to the ENDS, and negatively, or proscriptively to the MEANS through Executive Limitation policies.

In the ENDS and MEANS policies, a board's uniqueness is pleasantly expressed by, and because of, the diverse issues found spread throughout the various districts, and by the difference in the personal values of individual board members. One district might be extremely lenient with its superintendent, allowing him or her much latitude for making means decisions, while another may feel that its comfort zone demands more caution in the delegation of authority.

Trustee Domingo Carrillo of Premont ISD (personal conversation) expressed that the values of boards and staff personnel – and certainly those of teachers – from a large inner city school district might be quite different from those of a smaller district like his own. This difference in values is endemic to the American school scene and contributes to that refreshing diversity among boards.

However, when it comes to the governance process itself, if boards truly wish to make a difference, they cannot allow themselves quite the license for latitude as they can with issues and policies about ENDS and MEANS. This does not infer that all boards must march lock-step with each other and develop policies with identical wording and phraseology – just that the lenient expanse for responsible good sense is narrower when these important policies about how the board will govern itself are drafted.

Certainly, if a board's values lead it to choose different wording or ideological content, that is its prerogative; however, in the pursuit of excellence in governance, the structural design of the policy will not, and should not, vary from the suggested architectural examples created by Dr. Carver.

As such, the language used in the two remaining areas of policy – the Governance Process and the Board/Staff Relationship – tends to be somewhat cut-and-dried when compared with that of the previous categories, and finds itself repeated from board to board in much the same way as legalese lives and migrates in contracts and court proceedings. There is nothing wrong with this, as long as it is language that everyone understands.

One almost observes that the ideology of the next two categories of policy is academic, given their dependency on the effective distinction and utilization of ENDS and MEANS issues and policies about those issues – for everything here on out hinges on the cognizance of that concept. This does not make the wording of these policies any less profound or powerful, as the board's words must still say what they mean and mean what they say.

Policies about GOVERNANCE PROCESS

Governance Process policies are where the board will describe the methods by which it will govern the district and to impose upon itself the discipline necessary to do so. These policies spell out, first in broad terms and then through further definition, the board's accountability, its governing philosophy, and the product specifics of its own job.

As with the structural design of ENDS policies, this category is best drafted in outline form with an expandable preamble for each topic of policy, followed at each level by a more definitive elaboration. Unlike ENDS and Executive Limitation policies, it is the chairperson, not the superintendent, to whom the right is delegated for further interpretation of board policy. But, as with those other areas of policy, the chair must use – and demonstrate – logical reasoning when interpreting and further delineating what the board as a body has said.

"This category will begin with a very general overview statement of the board's commitment to govern through policy rather than through event-by-event decisions, and the board's recognition that board 'owns' the *school district* (my italicized insertion) on behalf of the community." (Carver/Mayhew, ANVOBL, ACCT 1994, p.55)

The primary Governance Process policy might read like this:

GOVERNANCE COMMITMENT

The purpose of governance is that the board, on behalf of the citizens of Faircity, guarantees the accountability of Faircity ISD by assuring that it (a) achieves appropriate results with the appropriate persons at an appropriate cost and (b) avoids unacceptable activities, conditions and decisions. In fulfillment of this charge, the board is committed to rigorous, continual improvement of its capability to define values and vision. (CGD Guided Policy Development packet)

This is quite a respectable stance, as it captures by the broad strokes of issue inclusion, those things that any board would be glad to claim as its governance commitment. However, none would be content with ending its statement of intent with so wide a latitude. Boards which commit themselves to Policy Governance want to further define the details of what that commitment means.

Attendant to this statement, the board will speak in greater detail to such things as:

1. The governing style the board will use, and its job description. (This subheading will embody that which Dr. Arzell Ball mentioned as a vital need of today's board, since it will describe the board job in terms of "value added", rather than in terms of busyness or activities; and it will also declare how the board will carry out its trusteeship connection with its owners. A board's success in making this link-up will ultimately determine its success in obtaining that much-coveted ownership input and its ability to communicate its values back to the ears of the community.)

2. Its planning cycle, and control of its own agenda.

3. The role of board officers including the president.

4. Committee principles and structure.

5. A board member's code of conduct. (This policy will in no way conflict with standing statutes which spell out State standards for ethics and conduct. It simply further defines how the board will conduct itself in its governance process, i.e., such things as interacting with administration and the public, conflicts of interest, meeting preparation, etc.)

As to its Governing Style, the board will say that it will govern with an emphasis on outward vision rather than an internal preoccupation; and that it will encourage diversity of viewpoint. It will center on strategic leadership more than administrative detail, and that it will seek a clear distinction of board and chief executive roles. (CGD Guided Policy Development packet)

Board Committee Principles Policy

"Perhaps the most deceivingly innocuous thing a board can do is to create a Board Committee."

That statement came not from the lips of a school board member, but was spoken by the mayor a small city. However, had it come from the president of a school board, the counsel would have been similarly wise. Board committees are vital to a board's performance and effectiveness; however, "Board Committees, when used, should be assigned so as to minimally interfere with the wholeness of the board's job and so as never to interfere with delegation from board to superintendent." (CGD Guided Policy Development packet)

Boards will read this admonition and scoff. "We would never do something like that," they might say.

Yet, these errors of governance are customarily committed by boards directly beneath their own diligent and well-intended noses. For example: Board committees are to help the board do its job, not to help the staff do its jobs. Neither should they be created to advise the staff. Yet how many times have we seen a board create an advisory committee whose job it is to give advice to the school superintendent?

As the veteran mayor alluded, this may seem so absolutely innocuous that boards do it without batting an eye. But the sinister climate it can spawn is far and away more detrimental than any good thing that can come out of it. For, consider the "chain of command" of the board/superintendent connection; and consider the board's agreement that all delegation will pass from the board to the staff through that same communication conduit.Consider also the advisory board's position in that chain of command, as it sits somewhere and advises the staff.

An advisory board is created by the board, which is the boss of the superintendent – whether or not that advisory group consists partly or entirely of board members or a mixture of trustees and citizens; therefore, it must be considered to have vested within it the authority of the board which created it. So, wherever it is located in the organizational chart, its station places it in a position of authority over the superintendent.

Now, we have a superintendent being advised by someone whose advice he must assume has the same weight of authority as if it were coming from the full school board, itself. What do we do when our boss gives us advice? We take it, of course.

When we consider the board's need to speak to the executive with one voice or not at all; and then visualize the position of command occupied by the advisory board, we can then see that the integrity of the one-voice principle has been compromised – and with it has been the watering down of accountability.

The solution is simple: If the staff wants advice, let it ask for it – and let it ask for it from whomever it chooses. It is possible that staff may choose to ask advice from someone on the board – after all, we elders who sit at counsel are not on the board simply because of our pretty faces. But likely as not they may decide to ask someone else.

When one wants advice, the option of choosing the advisor should be up to advisee; and if the superintendent needs advice, he may form as many advisory committees of his own as his heart's desire. These will be staff committees, not board committees; and the superintendent will be under no feeling of obligation to take whatever advice or recommendation is given by those groups.

Yet, Carver asks the plain question: "When was the last time you wanted advice on something and went to a committee to get it?"

Having said this, let me reiterate my earlier statement that board committees are vital to a board's performance...if they are created and used to do *Pre-board* work and not *Sub-board* work. Board committees – committees created by the board – should be created for the board. Their existence should be to assist the board in areas prerequisite to board deliberation and decisions.

An example of this would be a committee consisting of three trustees, or a combination of trustees and citizens, formed for the purpose of investigating the impact of consolidating two elementary schools versus raising the district tax rate. This would be a committee whose specific job was to obtain pertinent data and bring it back to inform the wisdom of the full board. The committee would be advised to bring – not its recommendation – but a list of options and alternatives, along with possible repercussions associated with the two avenues of choice. The committee would report its findings to the board, not the staff, as it is necessary information the board needs prior to making its leadership decisions.

Because the superintendent works for the full board,

these committees, either as individuals or as a group – and whether they be board trustees or not – cannot exercise authority over staff.

Role of the Chair

Now that the board has written and agreed on a policy saying it will center on strategic leadership and eschew administrative details, it is incumbent upon the board to adhere to its word. This particular policy gives the chair the right – and indeed the obligation – to quote the board's own words back to it when the inevitable allure of trivia tempts it from its agreed directive.

Where previously such admonition from the chair had to come from that person's own *belly of conscience*, this policy gives them fodder for the cannon of board leadership, to call to task any trustee who has trodden from the path of policy proviso and gotten off into areas which the board has agreed are off-limits.

Carver says the chair can now sing the board's own words back to it. *"These are your words, folks. This is the policy you adopted as a board. If you want to continue on this path of trivia, then you will have to modify your policy."*

Finally, the chairperson has a document in hand with which stern discipline – if that is what is called for – can be administered with the full validity of the board's own words behind it. Yet the board president's presence does not relieve other members from contributing to the integrity of the process. "The chairperson bears a peculiar responsibility with respect to board process; however, more cogent to this discussion, the entire board cannot avoid its share of responsibility." (John Carver, BTMAD p.138)

What Carver is implying is that in spite of written policy, there is no gun to the head of an undisciplined board. If the board as a whole does not accept its mature responsibility, the chairperson's presence and well-intended requests for regimen will result in nothing more than window dressing.

I don't wish to leave the impression that being the board's "sheriff" is the only duty of the chair. In fact, on a Policy Governance board it may be a duty of only passing importance. One of the most exciting aspects of a board which demonstrates its responsibility by every member feeling a duty to keep the group on track, is that the less difference it makes who the chair is. I can recall one client board whose president is hearing impaired to the extent he only reads lips and cannot be aware of the "wandering voices of trivia" that might arise beyond his vision. The board is a disciplined group thoroughly dedicated to the policies it has written; therefore, the "sheriff" has yet to toss a trustee in the *calaboose.*

Perhaps a more esteemed responsibility of the chair rests in that position's duty to further interpret the board's Governance Process and Board/Staff Relationship policies beyond the point at which the board as a body has stopped speaking. For that reason the board's choice of "Chair" is important, as that person must be able to use lucid thought in making a reasonable delineation of the board's intent in those two categories.

Board Job Description

In a previous chapter we related the simplicity of Dr. Rosenberger's five-point description of a board member's job. See how closely it relates to John Carver's suggested wording for that of a Policy Governance board:

The job of the board is to represent the public owner-ship (public, taxpayers, citizens) in determining appro-priate organizational performance. To distinguish the board's own unique job from the jobs of staff, the board will con-centrate its efforts on the following job "products" or out-puts:

1.   The link between the school district and its ownership.
2.   The production of written governing policies at the broadest levels.
3.   The assurance of Superintendent performance as judged solely against the criteria of those policies. (CGD Guided Policy Development packet)

It is this third point that concerns boards greatly, be-cause it goes to the heart of accountability. How can we be assured that our expectations are being properly ad-dressed and that nothing *untoward* is taking place in the performance of Executive duties?

To obtain this assurance, the board must monitor Ex-ecutive performance, not only because to do otherwise would not be a demonstration of good trusteeship, but because that's where the work takes place and the progress lies.

Monitoring policies will be drafted in the fourth and last area of board policy:

Policies about BOARD/STAFF Relationship

This category of policies describes how the board will connect with the administration and how authority is, and is not delegated to the superintendent. For instance, the master policy might say that the superintendent is accountable to the board as a body, not as individual board members. And that the board will speak with one voice or not at all.

Some State statutes allude to this arrangement without actually stating the finality of it – that the superintendent owes no heed to anything an individual trustee says (other than professional courtesy) unless it is said by the one-voice statement of the board as a body.

This firm stance, held in place by a written statement of policy, precludes much *leaky accountability* caused by trustees entering the superintendent's office by the "back door", and short-circuiting the board's full intent with personal agenda items and means suggestions of their own.

Haven't we all done it? Just ask someone with the administrative experience of a Superintendent Ball.

Secondly, the policy might say the board will instruct the administrator through its written ENDS and Executive Limitations policies, along with full delegation of interpretation. Further expansion of the board's intentions will fully establish the superintendent as "the single official link between board and staff" (Carver/Mayhew, ANVOBL, p.63), and define a job description for the superintendent.

This category will also include a statement, and possibly a schedule, specifying the board's intent to monitor organizational performance by judging it against the criteria established in its specific written policies (ENDS and Executive Limitations).

As with the policies of Governance Process, it will be the purview of the chairperson to make reasonable interpretive determinations in further advancing board policy beyond that which is drafted and adopted in this category.

Evaluating Executive Performance

I am reminded of a situation concerning a superintendent from a Mid-Texas school district. Like Raymond Doe, he wishes to remain anonymous, and Texas being such a vast state, I feel I am safe in narrowing his identity to this million square miles.

He had just completed his annual evaluation by the board, and he was not sure how well he had fared. He was aware of the nine items that his board had ostensibly graded him on, and had tried to envision how each of the members of the board might have evaluated him on them.

He said that during the evaluation he had sat patiently and listened as each trustee had expressed their opinion about a string of ambiguous and nearly impossible to measure indices; and that they all seemed to be as uncomfortable as was he. He tried to answer their questions with as much aplomb as possible, and they were as glad as he was when it was over.

He was being evaluated based on his job description "in concert with the criteria descriptors adopted by the State Board of Education". I asked him what that job description was, and he showed it to me. It was three pages long with nearly forty points on it. It looked like a self-improvement checklist for Lee Iacocca.

The Policy Governance Superintendent's Job Description

The type of job description John Carver recommends is one based not on a list of *busyness* items, but in terms of the unique outputs and responsibilities of the position. It is brief – almost as brief as the job description for the board:

"As the board's single official link to the operating organization, the superintendent's performance will be considered to be synonymous with organizational performance as a total." (CGD Board/Staff Relationship, Guided Policy Development packet)

The specifics of the policy might then use a wording

variance on the following:

The job contributions of the Superintendent, and, therefore the only things about which he/she may be evaluated are in two areas:

1. Organizational accomplishment of the provisions of board policies on ENDS.
2. Organization operation within the boundaries of prudence and ethics established in board policies on Executive Limitations.

It always goes back to ENDS and MEANS and their specific definitions under Policy Governance. That is why the ENDS/MEANS distinction is the single most important principle a board can master. The superintendent should be evaluated by (1) were the ENDS (stipulated and anticipated outcomes) accomplished to the board's satisfaction; and (2) were the stipulated boundaries of ethics and prudence in the Executive Limitations Policies not violated. If the answer to both those questions is "Yes", then the superintendent should get a passing grade. If the answer to either of them is "No", then perhaps the administrator should be asked to explain to the board why he or she should continue to be the administrator.

The patent answer boards give at this point is, "This is too easy. It's got to be harder than that." However, if the board has done its job first and drafted its policies in those two vital areas, telling the superintendent what is expected in the way of ENDS and what will not be acceptable in the way of MEANS, then what else is there to consider for evaluation?

Perhaps we should judge him by how close he shaves, or her by her adeptness in putting on makeup. Perhaps because of a perpetual smile, or always a cheerful word of greeting, etc.

Management skills? You bet. And if the ends were achieved and the limitations not violated, then the adequacy of those skills should not be in question.

However, if the superintendent is going to be held accountable for accomplishment of the outcomes – and it always comes down to that – then does it not also make sense to grade him or her fairly against that criterion? The nine points I mentioned that my friend was being judged against are certainly worthy areas of noting proficiency; yet, if one reads them, one can easily see that they are entirely about administrative means:

1. Instructional Management
2. School/organizational climate
3. School/organizational improvement
4. Personnel management
5. Administration and fiscal/facilities management
6. Student management
7. School/community relations
8. Professional growth and development
9. Board/Superintendent relations.

None of them address the question of whether or not something of benefit (what good for what people at what cost) was obtained by the school children of the district.

By the utilization of ENDS/MEANS criteria, in combination with regular, reliable monitoring information required by MONITORING policies, the superintendent is constantly evaluated against value standards that were set by the board. The executive report card is regularly upgraded by the fulfillment of reporting requirements generated by those very monitoring policies. The board can, therefore, see at a glance if the superintendent is getting good grades or poor. And so can the superintendent.

When time comes for that much-dreaded annual Superintendent Evaluation, all the board has to do is tally up the score and make its decision based on the question: "Were the board's stated ENDS fulfilled, and were all of its Executive Limitations complied with?

There is another vital point to this which I have not addressed, and which I want to do very delicately. That is, an evaluation system needs to guarantee the superintendent a "fair-shake" from all members of the board. As I said earlier, the job of the superintendent should not be a political one, but one of management and supervision. However, sometimes an administrator works for a board that is split between two ideological extremes. If the job is done properly and the majority decision of the board is adhered to, the superintendent may end up at odds with the remaining members – with whose values the superintendent may also disagree. When evaluation time comes, what are the chances the dissenters would grade the administrator high on such things as (1) his or her policy recommendation (either Liberally or Conservatively) about finance, instructional programs, and such things as student dress and other MEANS matters of the school district? Or (2) the way he or she might exercise judgment in matters not covered by board Policy?

Surely the superintendent's recommendations might be in conflict with members of opposing ideological viewpoints, and might not garner a good evaluation from their side of the aisle. This can become especially critical on boards where certain trustees typically try and "twist" the arm of the superintendent or inappropriately "bend his ear" in the office after board meetings.

Under the Policy Governance model, the superintendent would be evaluated only by whether or not the stipulated outcomes were achieved and the standards for prudence and ethics remained unsullied. Political or ideological leanings would have no bearing on the evaluation.

Monitoring Executive Performance

The simplicity of monitoring executive performance is so basic that I have purposely withheld it until this point. For as we have shown that evaluation of the superintendent is the same as evaluation of the district's progress, we can also say that in order to monitor the superintendent's performance, we must monitor those vital things about which the superintendent is *superintending:* That is, ENDS and MEANS, and specifically with regard to the limitations the board has imposed on those means.

If the board has cemented its clear governance role through its ENDS and MEANS policies, then "keeping up" with their progress in the right way is not a detriment to that leadership, but a demonstration of good stewardship. The important thing is for boards to monitor – or keep up with – all those things about which it has written policy; and to do so without getting into "means meddling" in the process.

Carver's definition of meddling has been stated as:
1. Jumping levels (remember the Chinese boxes analogy) into a much smaller area of concern than is the board's job to do, or
2. Prescribing the means by which the administration will do its job. If a board is not doing either of those, then it is not guilty of meddling; however, it still may not be using good monitoring methods.

Boards improperly monitor by nosing through piles of

staff documents (with staff's unwitting help and gratuitous supply) and anything else that might give it some insight into what is going on in the district. Carver describes this process as having ten-thousand answers, desperately in need of just a few good questions.

Another way boards have of monitoring is to attend to whatever wheel squeaks that particular month. If something seems to be atilt, then we'll attend to it and set it right. This is a variation on problem based solutions for board effectiveness; and it is neither a viable way of monitoring the district's nor the superintendent's performance.

Policy Governance suggests that the board look at monitoring in the larger context of: Since we know that we want to monitor ENDS outcomes and the compliance of Executive Limitations, what kind of information do we need to do so? Not all the information that comes to the board is necessary or helpful for monitoring, so let's first eliminate that kind of unusable information from our list.

Decision Making Information

Some of the information needed by the board is needed for planning. This is information that helps the board make its own decisions about things and get its job done. Such things as:

1. Information about trends
2. Changes in student and owner demographics, as that may likely effect the tax base
3. What are other organizations in the community aiming at?
4. Will we be duplicating what someone else is doing?

This information is prospective and non-judgmental. It looks to the future and informs the board's wisdom about what it must do to move the district forward.

Monitoring Information

Differing from decision-making information, *monitoring information* is both retrospective and judgmental. It looks to the past – to last year, or last month, or last week or yesterday if necessary; but it never looks to the future. As opposed to the other kinds of information the board will receive, monitoring information is target specific. That is, its interest is focused like the narrow aim of a rifle shot and is directly related to the superintendent's job, particularly with regard to compliance with ENDS and MEANS policies. For that reason, last month's financial statement is not an example of monitoring information.

Last month's financial statement tells the board only one thing for certain: that last month existed. Even at that, it still takes a vote by those members present to make it official.

An example of monitoring information would be: The board said it wanted students in *K through 6* to reach a certain level of competence in a particular skill or area of learning; did they get there? Or the board said the superintendent could not put long-term reserves at risk; did he do that?

As you can see, monitoring information is clearly judgmental and is data that should come to the board on a regular basis – per a monitoring policy and schedule. We will take up specific methods of obtaining that monitoring data after we deal with the last – and most prolific – kind of information the board receives.

Incidental Information

The general statement is that if it is not decision-making information or monitoring information, then it qualifies as incidental information. However, since it has been known to yield some insight in a very broad sense, incidental information often masquerades as the other two.

Good examples are lengthy reports on staff activities – with meticulous attention to detail of cost and performance – which come to the board and which are read and judged against no pre-set criteria for such cost or performance. Such "monitoring" is an illusion, with the board deluding itself and its ownership that it is staying on top of things. For, what standard is it monitoring this cost or performance against? What would not be acceptable?

Writes Carver (BTMAD, p.119), "Even the revered monthly or quarterly financial report stands indicted here. To the extent that the criteria against which the financial report is judged are not obvious, it yields incidental rather than monitoring information."

Carver concedes that, "Boards do, indeed get smarter in a scattered kind of way, but they wallow in information more than monitor with it. I have found that the majority of information received by boards is of this type."

There's nothing wrong with incidental information in itself; and if it helps a trustee feel more connected – as I pointed out in an earlier chapter – then it has its mild usefulness there. However, one of the major complaints of boards is that they have so much stuff to wade through that, "it could be a full-time job". Since most of the information that comes to a board is of this incidental type, if a board wishes to ease its reading burden, this is a legitimate place to start whacking.

A trustee's need to *feel connected* is an itch that cannot be scratched into submission, and the endless poring over incidental information is, therefore, a misplaced and inefficient remedy.

Boards that are deeply involved in the assimilation of

this type information have little time for visioning about the future of the district and creating policies to serve as criteria for judgment; and even if they did, the information itself is substandard for making any analysis of that performance.

Criteria for Monitoring

The relaxed feeling of assurance a board has when it knows it has good monitoring practices has been compared to the feeling a father has when he sends his teenage daughter out on her first date knowing that Grandmother is riding in the back seat. But that assurance by the board does not come without a price tag: the time spent preestablishing performance criteria through proactive policies.

This two-step board initiative of first creating clear criteria and then judging performance against that criteria is more than just a common sense management idea. It saves board time by allowing it to easily check results against clearly outlined expectations. It saves staff time by precluding false starts and re-dos because criteria were not clear in the beginning. It precludes unfair judgments of staff whose actions were initiated by well-intended administrators acting on what was assumed to be the criterion. It precludes gut-feeling judgments by trustees who may be influenced at the time of vote by personal idiosyncratic feelings to which other members are not privy.

We have all, at one time or another, been subjected to the ordeal of making judgments under personal duress. Perhaps our tax man had just called with bad news, or a sudden flare-up from that spicy dinner we knew better than to eat. Or the in-laws have decided to drop in for the weekend.

If a set standard lies on the table before the board, then judgment of staff performance against that standard is a better assurance of a fair and confident verdict.

Methods of Monitoring

Carver's admonition: "If you haven't said how it ought to be, don't ask how it is," directs a board to set policy and monitor against that criteria instead of trying to take in the entire panorama and hope it can spot something out of sync. The board can then use one or more of three suggested methods for doing this.

Executive Report

This is a report to the board that directly addresses whichever policy is being monitored according to the monitoring schedule. Carver's example (BTMAD, p.122) points out that the board's monitoring of financial condition would not be done via the familiar balance sheet and income statement; but would address the unacceptable circumstances specified in the policy on financial condition. The superintendent's report would state that he or she was either in compliance with the stipulations of that policy, or not. If in compliance, that affirmation should be immediately obvious by the presence of accompanying data. If such assertion is not clearly apparent to a majority of the board, so that it is reasonably assured of compliance, then the board has not received a monitoring report.

There are, of course, reasons – valid and otherwise – why a superintendent might not be in compliance with any given policy. And if so, that reason should be clearly part of the executive report for the board to read and consider.

External Audit

This is a method very familiar to schools, as they are accustomed to having an annual audit of their fiscal health; however, the external audit need not necessarily be of a financial nature. When using this method to monitor a policy, care should be taken that the outside judging party does so against criteria of the board's policy, and not against personal or professional trade standards he or she may have established for themselves.

Direct Inspection

One or more trustees are given the task of checking staff compliance with a certain policy. This method is simple but is only recommended in cases where the role of the board is clear to those doing the inspecting, and where proper discipline by those trustees can be assured. Care should be taken that "compliance" is judged only against the policy's criterion, based on a reasonable interpretation by staff. Improper use of this method occurs when the inspecting trustees overstep the monitoring intent and begin to prescribe or "meddle" in the means.

The dialogue should go something like this:

"George or Sarah (superintendent), according to the monitoring schedule it is time for the board to monitor Policy Number such-and-such. We want you to walk us through the implementation and employment of this policy."

George or Sarah would then show and explain to the trustees how the policy was being implemented according to his or her reasonable interpretation of that policy. The trustees should not call into question whether or not it is being done the way they, themselves, would do it if either were superintendent. But rather, their inspection should challenge the point of whether or not it is a reasonable interpretation.

If doubt arises as to the integrity of that interpretation, it would be the responsibility of the full board to resolve that doubt – not the several trustees who had made the inspection and raised the question.

CHAPTER NINE

A Bit About Budgeting

QUESTION: What does a Policy Governance discussion of school budget approval have in common with live fish bait? ANSWER: Both can be a can of worms.

In John Carver's Foreword to this text, he mentioned its "lighthearted" exposition in the same sentence with his applause for the book's integrity. John has known me for many years and understands that while I do not in most cases take myself too seriously, I do take the difficult jobs of board members very seriously.

It was for that reason that the first time I heard him present his views on the board's budget approval process, I hastened to say, "My goodness, John, isn't it enough that the concepts of Policy Governance are provocative in themselves. Now you had to go and tell the board that its practice of approving the budget is an empty symbol, a waste of time and a contribution to poor governance as well. Don't you realize that State law states affirmatively that the board must approve the budget?"

Certainly, Carver realized that. However, his contention is that simply because the legislature says the board must approve the budget is no guarantee that it makes for better control, or that it even makes good sense. Certainly, it makes good sense not to break the law; so, in that regard the board must do as it is told. Policy Governance does not recommend the board break the law. Instead, a smart board can find a way to obey the law and still not let it get in the way of good governance.

My statement is, that if the law says we must approve
the budget, then for Heaven's sake let's give it our bless-
ing and then get on with business. But unless we know
what it is we are approving – that is, against what specified criteria are we judging and approving the document
– then let's not delude ourselves into believing that it is a
demonstration of leadership. It's not. In fact, it's simple –
if there is such a word – *followship.*

However, school boards should be in the business of
leading. And, as *Final Authority,* when a board sits down
to approve a budget that someone else has initiated and
created based on that someone's vision of what that budget should look like, it is assuming a reactive stance. It is
reacting to the leadership initiative of someone to whom
it has unwittingly delegated the responsibility of deciding how much money will be spent by the district and for
what purposes. And the entity which has made those leadership
decisions – i.e., the staff – has assumed the superior role.

Boards will argue the stability of their leadership role
by saying that the approval process itself symbolizes that
strong position. But a symbol is all it is. By the time a
budget gets to the board a tremendous amount of staff time
(and money) is invested in it. When was the last time the
board actually disapproved the budget?

Oh, it's true that often times a board member will look
at a budget and comment that he or she thinks they ought
not to be putting so many resources into a certain index
of expenditure; and then two or three others will agree,
and there will be a revision. But if this is such an important item, then why was this allocation not made clear to
the superintendent before the document was put together. As often as not, these snap decisions are based upon
gut feelings at the time of approval – not judged against

solid initiative ENDS policy created to establish a standard of excellence in budgeting.

You will recall earlier where we said that the budget was only an administrative tool – a means to an end – and not something by which the district can be steered. The budget should not determine the board's vision for the district; instead, the vision should determine the budget. Boards have it all backward. The proper procedure is to (first) determine what the vision is, and (second) cause a budget document to be created which will facilitate the district's move toward that end.

Certainly, we're not talking about pie-in-the-sky visioning here. The board has the responsibility to look ahead with reason and sincerity in deciding its ENDS issues; and the drafting of all board ENDS policies invite the intelligent and experienced input of top administrative staff, as well as anyone else who can inform the board's wisdom. In creating the budget, few – if any – were ever put together in a closet anyway; and staff and board easily communicate any polarity that may arise between the board's vision and the reality of circumstance.

Aside from the addressing of ENDS, the budget that is approvable must also be able to withstand scrutiny in areas of prudence and ethics.

How is this assured under Policy Governance? By proper utilization of Executive Limitation policies, the board can easily dictate to its superintendent the characteristics it would find unacceptable in any budget brought before it. To do this, the board must first decide what those unacceptable traits are; and it does that by deciding the largest no-no first, and then coming in to the next largest, and then the next, etc., as we discussed in the chapter about formulating Executive Limitation policies. When a board does that, it finds there aren't many things it can list; but those that are listed represent the things, that if violated, could seriously jeopardize a superintendent's employment status.

Budget goals

What are some of those unacceptable things? Well, first, we know we don't want a budget that deviates materially from our board-stipulated ENDS, or that risks fiscal jeopardy, or fails to be derived from a multi-year plan. So, we write that down.

Next, we certainly don't want a budget that we can't read without professional guidance, do we; or one that is fiscally out-of-whack? So, we write that down, too.

The generic example of Carver Governance Design's Guided Policy Writing packet lists about five items that stipulate the kind of budget document that would be unacceptable to the board. And, by so doing, the board has effectively taken the leadership initiative and dictated what kind of budget it will approve (if it must) by stating what kind it *will not.*

Therefore, when the completed document comes to the table, the board can *monitor* it against its own specified initiative criteria which were set down in its ENDS and MEANS limitations. It can ask the pertinent questions based upon those criteria: Did our superintendent put our money where our mouths are (are our ENDS being properly addressed in this budget)? In so doing, were all of the executive limitations maintained in compliance?

If the answer to those questions is yes, then the budget should be approvable even if there was no quorum present on the night it was brought to the table. In fact, if the board's policies about budgeting have been complied with, the only thing that should keep THIS budget from bearing the stamp of approval before it even comes through the board room door would be if the board had CHANGED its POLICIES.

Obviously, before this process can take place, the board must first have done its job of deciding the ENDS issues to be addressed. In other words, we cannot ask if the superintendent has "put our money where our mouths are" until our mouths have first been somewhere. And we cannot ask if proper budgeting decorum was maintained until we first have decided the definition of *improper* decorum; i.e., our executive limitations. Once those hurdles are cleared, the budget is no longer a staff initiated document, but one whose structure is governed by the board.

The budget is a MEANS, not and ENDS; and the board has effectively dealt with it as it must with all such means issues.

So, the budget comes in, and the board sits down to monitor the document against the criteria of its policies – as good stewards should. To those watching in attendance, it looks for all the world like an approval process, doesn't it? So, who's to complain?

"What the Policy Governance model does is put the board's effort on the front end of the budgeting process rather than at the tail end. Let's admit that the budget is an administrative document. It's not a governance document at all." (Carver/Mayhew, ANVOBL, p.87)

Granted, the State Legislature pins the onus of budget approval squarely on the school board's back like a child's party game. But simply sitting down, looking at a document which has been initiated and created by staff prerogatives, and approving it against no specific criteria other than one's own gut-feeling is not leadership.

See, I told you it was a can of worms.

CHAPTER TEN

"GOVERN LIKE YOU MEAN IT"

Implementation of the Policy Governance model, that is the institutionalization of its principles, requires serious board deliberation. A board should never make the decision to begin using the model simply because a lot of other people are doing it. It should fully understand its reason for deciding to make the leap of faith.

"Unless the board is convinced that there is a need for better governance, any changes are going to be cosmetic." (Carver/Mayhew, ANVOBL, p.123)

For with the decision to get on line, is the need for dedicated commitment to organizational excellence. The board must be willing to take part of Raymond Doe's suggestion: That is, keep the goose, but throw out the sauce and start cooking anew.

It has been our experience that once a board learns the new paradigm concepts, it can effectively draft new policies for needs which arise during its tenure. Nothing succeeds like success; and the best way for a board to assure continuance of Policy Governance principles is to use them and pass them on to posterity. With proper discipline and good orientation of new members, the system endures to meet the governance needs of future boards that are seated.

We have no way of knowing how many boards have learned of the Policy Governance model from available literature and have adopted it as their own. We assume those groups had the time available to complete the necessary policies in the four categories of governance need: ENDS, Executive Limitations, Governance Process, and Board/ Staff Relationship.

For those who do not have the time – nor inclination to spend it writing policies over a protracted period – a guided session with a qualified Policy Governance consultant would be a viable alternative. For this is something that should not be half-done.

Carver uses the amusing comparative portrayal of a country deciding to change its traffic laws from having vehicles drive on the left-hand side of the highway to having them drive on the right – and staging it in gradually.

This week trucks, and next week the cars.

MOVE AHEAD OF THE PACK

Fielding the Leadership Team

I once visited with a superintendent who told me with pride that his job was to be the driving locomotive for the district. Yet, when I witnessed this administrator struggling to put his train on the same tracks as those of his board, it appeared as if everyone wanted to be the caboose.

The board and the superintendent constitute a leadership team. As I have shown, their roles are separate – though entirely supportive of each other. In the game of boardsmanship – as in those of athletic competition – the team can function only so long as the position each plays is clearly defined and properly maintained.

As the first baseman must be certain that the right fielder will not come rushing in to shag a slow grounder, so also must the superintendent be assured that the board will deal with matters of governance without getting "out of fielding position" and into matters of management. Likewise, the board must have confidence in its superintendent to deal with and resolve management issues "while respectfully staying out of governance". (Carver BTMAD, p.128)

Dr. Rosenberger once drew an impossible analogy of a team trying to play football on a field with the goal posts placed randomly around an irregularly shaped area. Carver has purposed the incongruity of men playing football with baseball rules. Try to imagine a group of kids playing hide-and-seek with nobody selected to be "it".

Well thought-out State statutes, innovative training programs by the Associations of School Boards and School Administrators, and school board bylaws, have combined to make boards keenly aware of the nature of their team roles. Policy Governance suggests we take it a step forward.

"Governance (Carver – A New Standard of Governance for Public Education) is not about budget lines, personnel issues and field trip approvals. It is about values and vision and strategic leadership. The re-invention of the school board calls for a new paradigm, a fresh reconstruction of what the work of the board is to be."